TERRY PRONE

Just
a few
Words

BUSINESS
POOLBEG

First published by Turoe Press, Dublin, 1984
This edition published 1989 by
Poolbeg Press Ltd
Knocksedan House,
Swords, Co Dublin, Ireland
Reprinted 1993

A catalogue record for this book is available from the British Library.

ISBN 1 85371 031 8

Author photograph by Mac Innes Photography
Cover design by emSpace
Printed by The Guernsey Press Company Ltd,
Vale, Guernsey, Channel Islands

Also By
Terry Prone

Write and Get Paid for It
Do Your Own Publicity
Be Your Own Boss (with Frances
Stephenson)
Get That Job

BUSINESS
POOLBEG

For Tom 143 x 14

Contents

Chapter 1

Talking in Public—
the changes made by television and radio

It is a curious phenomenon that in this glacial era of
computers which we are just entering, it is warmth and
warmth alone that succeeds on television.

Peter Ustinov

Television and radio have made radical changes in the nature of
an audience's expectations of a speaker whether they encounter
that speaker through their TV screens, their radios or as
entertainment following a corporate dinner. Television has not
just changed the way we talk *on television* it has radically
changed the rules for all public speaking. The result is that
traditional wisdom about eloquence and oratory needs re-
evaluation. The problem is that many speakers do not do that
and disappoint the expectations of today's audiences by
hanging on to a kind of public speaking that belongs in the last
century, and by following outdated advice. Advice like
"Pretend your audience is a row of cabbages and relax." Advice
like "Mark the places on your script where you'll make
gestures." Advice like "Pause for three seconds at this point."
Advice that has been made obsolete by the intimacy of
television.

Public communication used to be a matter of Us and Him Up
There. Now, it's Me and You. Me at home watching my 26"
version of you.

Come into my home and address me like a row of cabbages

and I will go make myself a cup of tea, because if there is one thing none of us can stand, it is to be treated as a tiny constituent of some amorphous listening mass. Queen Victoria once said that the reason she did not like Gladstone was because he addressed her as if she were a public meeting.

Not only will people not listen if on radio or TV they are talked to as if they were conglomerate millions, but, assuming a group leaves the comfort of its home to listen to a speaker in the local hall, it is not going to behave differently. The individuals in that group and Queen Victoria will still be of one mind, and it is that one mind that the speaker has to talk to. Civilly. Entertainingly. Unpompously. Directly. And honestly.

But how many people end up talking in public, or appearing on radio or television? The numbers are surprisingly large. One of the peripatetic radio or TV programmes comes to town and several people are interviewed. Or a strike breaks out in the area, and the news media descend. Or someone from the area gets tickets for a TV discussion programme and perhaps wins a chance to speak. Community radio also absorbs people. Here facilities are put at the disposal of local groups for a week or so, during which they provide their own programming ideas and personnel. Local radio provides opportunities for many more. And where radio goes, television tends to follow, so it can be assumed that the precedents set in local, community and pirate radio, will be developed in due time by television.

One thing is certain. Talking in public to groups of people, or appearing before the microphones to make a particular point has become a regular necessity to a great number of people. With the growth of special interest groups, the likelihood is that more of us will be appearing in public in the future, either on platforms or in studios. Which is all to the good. There is always the chance that something valuable which one person says might influence a great many more people. There is every hope that we will discover more and more interesting and entertaining personalities to watch. From the point of view of the person appearing, TV pays moderately well and it is pleasant when the taxidriver asks for your autograph.

TV and radio are not, however, the only areas in which the need for good communication is important. Increasingly, people involved in community groups, sports, arts, crafts, politics, education and other live issues are under pressure to talk in public and to do it well. That public talking may involve radio and television. But it may not.

Even if it does not, the impact of radio and television is important. People are used to the directness and speed of television presentation, and this in turn may affect the way in which an argument should be put to the public in the local hall, the annual conference or at the street meeting. It may affect the method of communication by raising specific questions: "Do we need to commission a film? Slides? A video programme?" "Can we let the chairman waffle on or should we circumscribe him in some way?" "Should we do it as a twohander or singly?" It certainly should affect the preparation of the people who will do the talking.

This book is about coping with the changed nature of public communication wrought by the mass media, to help speakers do as good a job for twentieth century listeners as the great speakers of the past did for eighteenth and nineteenth century listeners.

It has to be recognised, however, that there are some people who have neither the desire nor the potential to communicate this well. Some people cannot do it because of the nature of their jobs. Business people are often successful to the extent that they can keep their mouths shut and their thoughts to themselves. If they reveal the details of a proposed merger, they may knock the profitability out of it. Some people cannot do it because of the nature of their upbringing. They have always been taught that keeping all available information to yourself gives you power and keeps the barbarians at the gates, and so they are constitutionally secretive, even when there is no secret within ten miles of them. Public information sharing is a physical agony for them, and it shows. Some people cannot do it because they have a contempt for the process. Sharing ideas and information with others butters no cabbage with them. If it must be seen to be done, then some naive front-person can be bought into the PR department, wound up, and set going.

People who have a contempt for media, a horror of a live audience or an inbuilt revulsion for the business of public communication should stay out of it. There are consequences. Someone else will step into the spotlight. If one entrepreneur will not appear on the TV money programme, another will, and if the replacement is a good TV performer, he will reap a disproportionate share of the available publicity. This, however, will not make enormous changes in the saleschart of either company.

The important thing is to decide either to go or not to go. And, having decided (if you do so) to go, to commit yourself to the going with a positive frame of mind and proper preparation. A defensive person with loser written all over him invites a tough interview and repels the viewer.

The vital pre-requisite of a good performance, in addition to willingness, is preparation. Preparation means writing for the spoken word, as opposed to producing something which would fit elegantly on the leader page of *The Times*. It means freshness —you cannot use the joke a comedian used on last week's Royal Variety programme. Television has changed public speaking in many ways, but this is perhaps the most ruthless way—it eats material. Comedians in the past could make a good living for years out of three sketches. Three sketches do not even fill one television programme today, and afterwards, those three have been sucked dry for good.

Preparation is part of the challenge of post TV communication. It helps to lessen the fear, to control the unpredictable, to reduce boredom. Preparation is the key to good communication.

Chapter 2

Before You Open Your Mouth

His misfortune in conversation is this: he goes on without
knowing how he is to get off.

Dr Johnson on Oliver Goldsmith

You may have been seeking the opportunity. You may have
been avoiding it like the bubonics. But when you are invited to
speak publicly, your first reaction should be neither delight nor
terror. Your first reaction should be to ask questions, because
until you have all of the relevant information about the
appearance you are invited to make, you cannot prepare
adequately. Without preparation, you cannot give a
professional performance.

So let's start with the key questions you will need answers to:

Who Am I Talking To?

You do not give the same speech to an audience of charitable
volunteers as you do to a group of captains of industry. You do
not give the same speech to a technically knowledgeable
audience as you give to people who are initiates to a subject. If
you are talking to a fairly general audience, that is a different
situation to the one which obtains if you are asked to appear
before a University debating society. It is a watchword of good
communications that you always start with the customer. It
helps if you know who the customer is.

How Many Will be There?

Talking to a very large group (more than 300 people) is a vastly different task than talking to twenty people. If it is a large group, then you need to know about microphones, podiums and the lighting involved. You also need to get there in advance, so you can personally check each of these technicalities. Not so long ago, I watched a keynote speaker approach a podium which was so tall, relative to his less than average height, that it made him look like an anxious child peering over a school desk at a classroom full of teachers. The impression was reinforced when the microphone, turned on, delivered itself of screams appropriate for nuclear explosion warnings. When the microphone had been mollified, the speaker then timidly addressed his script. It was clear to the first few rows of seating that the lighting was inadequate, but at this point the speaker, defeated by events thus far, kept going.

The end result was a disaster. Audiences, although they have a marvellous humorous patience with well-handled problems on the part of the speaker, have no sympathy whatever with someone who is not coping in public. In this instance, the speaker walked himself into all of his problems by not checking out the key inanimate factors that influenced his address before he got launched.

If you are third speaker in a daylong seminar, then you have fewer worries on this score. The earlier speakers will, in effect, have done your microphone and lighting tests for you. I would still recommend that, if you can, you go to the room where the speaking is to be done the previous night and go through your material so that you are comfortable when the time comes to do it for real.

Asking in advance about the numbers can give you some control, too. Some people, filling a hall with 300 seats, will leave a large gap between the first seats and the stage or the platform from which the speakers will speak. The end result is that speakers cannot even *see* those they are supposed to be relating to.

In similar vein, if you have smaller groups—twenty or fewer

people—you may want to contribute to the plans for how they are going to be seated. There are four basic possibilities:

1. Theatre Style

Theatre style seating is OK for large groups, but is much less effective for smaller numbers, as it tends to get in the way of a developing group dynamic and makes the passing of materials from hand to hand tedious. It is, however, acceptable for small numbers if you are showing visual aids which are best view from directly in front, if all of the detail provided on those visuals is to be seen with equal clarity by all those present.

2. Classroom Style

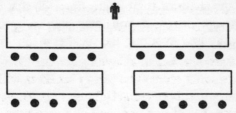

This is a variant on Theatre Style, the extra element involved being desks. It is bluntly hierarchical and recognisable as such. In one of the training rooms in my company's premises, this set-up invariably stops incoming executives in their tracks.

"Oh, back to school," one of them will say ruefully. For that reason, we tend to use it only when people are being briefed for subsequent exercises, and we are imparting information to help each individual deliver on a task, as opposed to focusing on developing relationships within the group, sharing information between group members or achieving teamwork. Like the

Theatre Style room configuration, this is useful if you want all present to have equal, or nearly equal, visual access to your flip chart or slide screen.

3.The Picture Frame

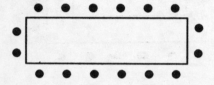

The moment I see the sketch for this room configuration, I recall great corporate fights which took place across the gap in the middle of the desks. I have no idea why it is, but this configuration tends, in my experience, to create awkwardness and division rather than teamwork or cooperation. To be avoided if possible.

If you must talk to a picture frame group of people, see if you can influence the share of the picture frame so that it slightly favours the speaker, even if you later plan to involve each member of the group. Favouring the speaker means putting the chairs thus:

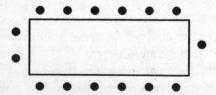

It is clearly hierarchical, but it does mean that while you are speaking, you are not worrying that people close to you on left and right might be reading your notes and getting the joke before you get to it.

4. The Horseshoe

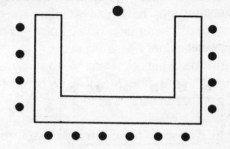

This is one of the most effective, in that it allows the group to develop into a team, and it allows a mobile speaker to move into and out of the horseshoe to emphasise particular points or involve particular people. A horseshoe involving more than fifteen people, however, begins to be unwieldy. More than 22 people and it becomes more of a hindrance than a help.

No matter what the physical set-up is, the one thing you can be sure of (unless, of course, you are third speaker in a continuous day of speeches) is that there will be late comers. This is a problem which can be minimised by good planning.

Let us say you have a theatre configuration. Ask, in advance, that the final row of chairs be withheld. This will mean that as the room fills up, people tend to move into the front seats and fill them up, which in itself is a good thing. Talking to a half empty first three rows is not one of life's great experiences. This arrangement also means that as you walk to the podium, the final row can be put out and will sit there, invitingly empty, for the late arrivers to slink gratefully into.

In a similar vein, if you are using the classroom or horseshoe configurations and you know, when the time has come for the session to start, that there are two people who still have not arrived, you should do two things. You should firstly ask the people nearest the door to move away and leave empty seats there, on the basis that the latecomers will disrupt things a bit less if they do not have to fall all over everybody else *en route* to their seats. You should secondly ask for the names of the

9

latecomers. This allows you to preempt a disruptive inevitability, which is that when the latecomer arrives, everybody figures out who he is and wonders what you, the speaker, think of him arriving late. If you know his name, you can glance up when the door opens.

"Hi, you must be Michael Dunn?" you say smilingly. "You're welcome. You'll find a seat over here on the left. Where we had got to, Michael, was to a discussion about the statistics on yield for 1992."

A potential distraction is turned into an asset, the way an oyster goes to work on a bit of grit.

Where is the Event?

Oh, come *on,* I hear you say. You don't really have to ask obvious questions like that in order to give a good speech, do you? Sorry, you do. One client of mine was late for his slot on a complex programme because he made the assumption that the event was to take place in the hostelry where the previous nine in an annual series had happened. Uh, uh, gotcha, they had shifted the location. Did he feel a fool? Yes. Did he deserve to? Yes, Did it disimprove his performance? Yes.

Every now and again, people organising a conference do a superb job of giving speakers the information they need. I recently received from an organiser a three page brief, Faxed to my office a week in advance. It gave me the address and telephone number of the conference centre, a sketch or simple map and a series of street directions which turned out to be foolproof, because I was the fool and I can misunderstand most maps if you give me time. It estimated the time taken for the journey accurately and gave an indication of where within the conference the event was to take place. Such briefings are rare. Since you cannot assume that they will be provided, you need to ask all of the questions given in this chapter.

What Time of the Day is the Speech Happening?

It matters. Being the first speaker in a day long conference is a different proposition to being the final after-dinner speaker.

Being the after-lunch speaker means that you are in what's called the Dead Hour. When people fall asleep unless you scintillate. Being an early morning speaker on the second day of a conference is particularly exigent, because half of those present are likely to be hungover. One conference organiser recently solved this particular problem by scheduling a gruelling current-affairs-type interview with his two top managers for the after-breakfast session on the second day. Their subordinates watched, amused, stimulated and, best of all, *awake*, as a TV interviewer lashed the two managers through a contentious question and answer session which left both of them feeling that they had undergone a public drubbing, but which in fact allowed them to articulate points which might have been lost in the predictability and boredom of a normal second day opening presentation.

Once you know the time you're scheduled for, you know how early to arrive. The ground rules are simple. You need to arrive with time to spare. Not as one client of mine arranged it, with four minutes of his time already elapsed. What happened in this instance was that the client decided to absent himself from his staff conference for a couple of hours in order to close a big deal, which he did. He failed, however, to remember the roads he had travelled, and so even though he broke every available speed limit, he still managed to arrive breathless and a little late. That was the physical reality. The less obvious mental reality was that he had no sense of what he was there to say or what were his presentation priorities.

"I survived it, just about," he told me afterwards. "And I'll never, ever do it again. You must have time to get your head together before you go up on a platform to talk."

On the other hand, you should not arrive so far in advance of your allotted time that you end up being sucked into conversation and being given other tasks. Arrive in time to retreat to a room on your own. This may be your hotel room, if you are staying overnight, or, if the worst comes to the worst, the loo. Read through your notes. Concentrate on what you are going to do. Get your mind attuned to the task in hand and then go out there and kick 'em dead. *Never* go to a podium distracted by recent conversation and without a clear sense of what your opening statement is.

What Does this Audience Want to Know

Too often, public speakers set out to tell an audience, not what that audience needs to know, but what the speaker believes the audience *should want to know*. Which is a little bit like talking to three year old about the nutritional value of boiled sweets. Of course, theoretically, if your average three year old knew about the damage sugar does to teeth and weight, that three year old might swear an oath of allegiance to raw carrots or apples. But it doesn't work that way. If you want a three year old to hear *anything* you have to say, you have to find ways of making it interesting to the three year old. You have to start where the three year old is.

It's the same exercise with an audience. You have your body of material there beside you. In order to decide which bits to bring with you and what shape they should be in, you have to work out where the audience is. One British nutrition activist addressed this problem when she realised that starting a talk by directing each adult to pay attention to the list of contents on the back of processed food packages was not working. Audiences gazed at her with dumb resentment.

So she went back to the drawing board. What did this audience she was due to address next week actually eat? A bit of research yielded the top four brand names. On the next public occasion, she arrived on stage with an armful of cartons.

"There may be someone here today who doesn't eat one of these," she said, plonking them down on a centre stage table while she talked and turning each of them so that its brightly identifiable face was to the viewers. "But I wouldn't bank on it. Most of us eat one of more of them. Now, let me show you what we get when we eat these things."

At this point, she stumped off the stage and came back with two bowls and a bottle. One bowl held lard full to overflowing. One bowl held sugar piled into a central mountain. The bottle held something liquid. These were plonked in front of the packages, while she explained that if we ate product A, we swallowed this much sugar per week, this much hidden animal fat, and this much preservative. By the time she reached Product D, the audience were alive, responding and understanding something with a vividness they had never expected from a lecture. The lecturer had also become less nervous, because she was so concentrated on not spilling things and on taking the audience through the implications of the contents of the containers she was using as visual aids that she had forgotten how frightened she was.

You do not have to bring props to a speech, but you *do* have to bring an instinct for what people really want to know about your subject.

When in doubt, ask. Ask the organisers what they believe people want to know about. I offer this advice with a built-in caveat. Many of those who organise conferences or who book public personalities haven't a clue what an audience actually wants. They say things like "Just be yourself," which has to be the least valuable advice ever offered.

There is one important negative aspect of finding out in advance what an audience wants to know about. It may indicate to you that you are the wrong person to deliver the speech. In which case, indicate that you are not suited to this particular occasion, suggest an alternative speaker, and stay home watching TV.

Is there a panel, and if so, who's on it?

Every now and again, a speaker turns up for a public occasion to discover that the platform he assumed was devoted exclusively to him is occupied by a panel of three speakers. Or worse still, that there are six speakers on stage, three of them opposing the points he had planned to make, and two of them (in addition to himself) promoting those points.

Ask in advance about who is on the platform, what they are doing there, and in what order they will speak. If you are covering a topic which is to be addressed by other speakers, then you should have, in advance, some notion of what those other speakers want to say. Without that knowledge, you are likely to duplicate what they say and leave other matters unattended to. If there is someone on the platform with whom it would be inappropriate for you to appear (and there are occasions when, politically or corporately, this might be the case) then you should bow out early enough for them to find a substitute.

What Language is Spoken by the Audience?
If you are appearing overseas, or at a major international conference at home, it may be that the majority of the audience will not have English as their mother tongue, in which case there are two options for the speakers. The first option is that of simultaneous translation. This is where a group of translators sit in booths and voice a translation of what you are saying which is fed to earphones worn by audience members. The translation is always a beat or two behind the speaker, which is unnerving, because if you make a joke, the laugh comes about twenty seconds later than it normally would.

When simultaneous translation is being planned, a script can be very helpful to the translators. Meeting them in advance can help too, if you plan to divert from the script at any time. Meeting them allows them to come to terms with your speech patterns and to get some flavour of the digressions you may take from the text as typed. It also affords them the opportunity to seek clarification on technical terms.

Where there is not a simultaneous translation, but where the audience is not uniform in its understanding of the language you are using, you must watch the audience with even more attention than is normally required. Audience members tell you visibly when they do not follow a point you are making. The immediate, classic response is that of the British tourist overseas, who says the same thing again, but slower and louder the second time around. Talking slower is rarely the solution to this problem. Indeed, there *is* no general or easy solution. However, in preparing your material before you make your appearance, you should seek to remove from it any slang or jargon which will not be readily understood. In training high-tech salesmen in the US, I have found that, even though we share the same language, every now and again I will use a phrase which is very Irish, although still in the English language, and blank faces break out all round me.

The second consideration is to illustrate the points you are making, rather than use more words. Concepts are much more easily understood when presented in pictures or stories. (See page 25). This applies to the power of ten when you are speaking to people who do not share your language. If they are puzzled by the words you use first time around, paint a different picture using differing words, and they are likely to climb aboard with great relief, as opposed to the irritated look of "please don't patronise me just because I don't understand" which is more likely to cross their face if you merely talk more s-l-o-w-l-y.

If there is any doubt about the capacity of the participants to understand, then do not take on the assignment. This is bitter experience talking. Tom Savage (my husband) and I were asked ten years ago to give two days media training to a group of Arab students. Sure, we said. No bother. Mother tongue? Not English, they said, but there would be two translators present. Mmm, we said. Oh, no, the translators would never leave the room, the organisers said. It would be fine. Grand. Perfect. Dead easy.

We arrived. Thirty students (we had been told to expect fourteen) gazed at us out of startlingly dulled eyes. One of the translators explained that this was the feast of Ramadan, so they could not eat during the hours of daylight. As a result, they had booked the hotel staff to cook through the night, and once dusk had fallen, had gotten down to some serious eating. They were now stuffed and sleepy.

The translator who brought all this to our notice was slow and halting, and this worried us. However, we figured that, in combination with the other man, he might be reasonably competent. The other man arrived.

"How you do to?" he asked us, bowing. We thought about this for a while, and figuring that he was asking us how did we do, we told him we did nicely thank you. How did he do?

"Ah, yes," he said in breathy consensus. What we did not know was that we had just exhausted his full repertoire of English phrases. An hour later, we were trying to teach the subtleties of mass media to a group of comatose foreigners in a language they could not understand. What was most disturbing about the whole thing was that it was perfectly clear that they preferred this kind of education. One by one they went to the back of the classroom to sleep, leaving a front row of apparently attentive blank faces, each of which, when addressed directly, said "Ah yes," with civil non-comprehension.

Do you understand the point I have just made?

Ah, yes.

Are you ready for us to make progress?

Ah, yes.

Would you like me to murder and parboil your mother?

Ah, yes.

Moral? Get a realistic estimate of the language competence of the audience and plan accordingly.

How Long Are You Expected to Talk For?

Believe it or not, the answer to this is likely to be "too long." People planning a day's speeches think in hour long chunks or half hour long chunks. People asking you to address their annual dinner often assume you will talk for an hour.

Very few people are good for an hour. In the old days of vaudeville, there was a rigid rule which said that no act went on for longer than twelve minutes. The old vaudeville players watched their audiences. They had to—turn your back in the middle of an act that was not going well, and you found yourself spattered with rotten tomatoes, brought for the purpose of showing disapprobation. Many people who could be very good for twelve minutes find themselves fitting into time slots of sixty minutes, and they fail to fill those time slots. They may not finish too soon, but their content and energy runs out long before the hour is over. Influence the people inviting you to allow you to speak for the appropriate length, rather than the length that fits the hotel's coffee breaks. Your personal comfort level matters. If you know that after a half hour you die on your feet, then, if forced to talk for an hour, you will begin that dying process from the word go.

What's the Context?

This may be something you can work out for yourself, rather than have someone tell you. What you're groping towards is an understanding of the atmosphere which will obtain in the venue when you stand up to speak. Are the people going to be grim and eager for some kind of break in the routine? Are they going to be tired of the introductory pieces and eager for someone who will give them real meat? If you have some knowledge of the atmosphere, you know where to start your speech. Perhaps the best example of this was more than a quarter of a century ago, when the late President Jack Kennedy was addressing a major foreign policy briefing for US ambassadors gathered in Washington. Speakers outlined the global situation, the threats facing American interests in various international arenas and the weaknesses in the management of American influence worldwide. The atmosphere was serious, the content was detailed, and by the time the President arrived the participants were a little worn.

The President arrived, tanned and tropically dressed from a holiday in plush Palm Beach, Florida. He stood before the palefaced gathering and was silent for just a moment.

"I know that you have been listening to Secretary Rusk and other experts all day, telling you the difficulties we face all around the world."

Small pause.

"Well, I'm here to report that the situation in Palm Beach is stable!"

The laugh allowed for release of tension, warmed up the audience and in no way detracted from the very serious material he then offered. He had worked out in advance precisely where

^

...ce was at, and met their unspoken needs.

...do I Want to Achieve?

H...stly now? Do you just want to survive? To fill time with words? Is your ambition limited to the desire to leave them with a positive personal impression? ("He looked and talked well. No, I don't remember what he actually said but you could hear every word and he didn't spill his glass of water.")

Talking in public is a strain. To do it properly requires hours of preparation and a certain amount of personal stress. So why do it, unless you plan to achieve something by so doing? Ideally, you should be aiming at a more professional performance. But more important, you should have a clear notion of what you want the people there to remember when you have finished. Not just the illustrations you used; you should want to change people's minds, improve their understanding, enlighten their comprehension of whatever it is that you are talking about. If the individuals present go home and say over the suppertime cup of tea "Do you know, your man said a very interesting thing today...", what do you want that interesting remembered thing to be? If one of your audience was forced to make a 30-second summary of what you talked about, how would you want that individual to summarise your speech?

In addition to remembering what you said, it is marvellous when you leave an audience with a sense of something they must *do* whether that is write to their public representative, change their lifestyle or join Amnesty International. Good speeches make people think. Great speeches change lives.

OK, I know what I want to achieve. Now, How do I do it?
See chapter 3.

Is it going to be a straight speech or a speech followed by questions and answers?
If questions are to follow your speech, then in preparing your material (see pages 32 to 34) you should not provide all of the

answers. Seek the clouds a little. Drop hints. Raise issues but ,
not put every concern to bed in your main text. Make references
to the question and answer session which is due to happen later
on..

When the person in the chair, at the end of your speech,
announces that it is time for the audience to ask questions, there
is a built-in hurdle which should be eliminated in advance.
Asked to put questions, an audience will do one of two things.
The first is that someone will speak who has been stimulated so
much by the speech that they are dying to ask questions. Or
someone who brought their very own axe with them to grind.
Once they have got the thing going, others will follow.

On the other hand, there is too frequently a situation where
the audience is stricken with apparently terminal silence. When
this happens, these options are usually taken up, when they
should *always* be rejected. The first one is that the speaker who
feels reproached by the group silence, decides that he is
responsible for filling it, and so he gets launched all over again
on his speech. The second one is that the chairman is goaded
into taking on the interviewer role, and, blanked of real
questions from the audience, asks whatever comes into his
head. This never turns out to be what the audience wanted to
have asked, and the development of a real interaction between
audience and speaker is postponed indefinitely.

Speaker and Chair should discuss this in advance and come
to an agreement that when questions are invited from the
audience, neither of them will fill the silence. This places the
onus of speech onto the audience, and within forty seconds
somebody breaks the hush with a question. The forty seconds
are hell for both speaker and chair, but they are effective, and
quickly forgotten. If the interval goes on for a minute or so, the
Chair (NOT the speaker) should make some flattering comment
to the effect that the speaker evidently answered all of the
questions the audience brought with then, and he is therefore
going to wind up the night's proceedings. At this point, wilting
violets tend to unwilt and say in a cheated tone that they DID
have a VERY important question to ask, in which case the Chair

n to ask it. If violets stay wilted, the Chair invites
he speaker and we all go home earlier than we
remember, as speaker your job is to make a
swer questions. Not take responsibility for filling
every silent moment. If you are in the Chair, your job is to keep
things moving, not transform yourself into a second-rate
interviewer.

In handling audience questions, these are the priorities:

1   Everybody Must Know what the Question Is
If you take a question from the front row, the people in the
back may not have heard it. Repeat all positive questions.
Paraphrase negative ones, taking any particularly obnoxious
words out, unless you can have a little fun with them.

2   Treat Every Question Equally
When a third questioner asks you a particularly good
question, it is very tempting to tell him so. The problem is
that questioners One and Two then feel that they have been
rubbished. Each question is new, challenging and
stimulating.

3   Use Chances to Repeat Points
Every now and again, you'll be asked a question the answer
to which was incorporated in your speech. This happens
because no one person in the audience will listen and hear
each point equally. All of them will go mentally walkabout
at some stage—you must pray they do not all do it together
and at the stage when you are making your most crucial
input. When someone asks you a question to which the
answer is obvious and already on the table, welcome the
opportunity to repeat yourself (TV ads go on dozens of time
each night because ad agencies know the value of
repetition). Find a way to illustrate the point so that the
covering of the same ground does not become an irritant to
the others present.

4 Keep Nodding To a Minimum

You may be indicating that you understand what you are being asked. Nodding may give people the impression that you agree with what is being asked which may not be the case at all. Nodding in any case is an overused physical method of communication. You can end up looking like one of those toy animals some drivers put on the back windowsill of their cars, and which have heads that go up and down in mesmeric response to the movement of the vehicle.

5 Don't Go On Too Long

Questioners should be thought of as asking for a drink—not seeking immediate delivery of Niagara Falls.

6 Do Watch Your Questioner

Too few speakers do. No questioner from the audience should be left with an answer to a question he did not intend to ask or 60% of an answer when 100% was what he (and those of the audience who understood the thrust of his query) needed.

7 Do Take Blame

If you get the wrong end of the stick, say so. When someone points out that you did not answer the second part of Joe Bloggs's query, say you are so sorry to Joe Bloggs, is there any chance he would tell you again what he wanted to know?

8 Do Listen

Wait until the end of a question. Where a questioner is verbose, it is all too tempting to jump in, tell him you know where he's going, and begin to answer his question. Don't do it. Listen with concealed patience. Unconcealed patience is arguably more insulting than being bluntly interrupted.

Finally, look at the sections in this book which deal with

Some of what is suggested as preparation for
ved is also relevant when it comes to speeches
e followed by interaction with a live audience.

Do I Need to Invest in Public Speaking Courses?

I don't know. I don't know your audience, your subject, how
often you will need to talk, what your personality is like, and
what sort of thought pattern you operate. In general, approach
training programmes in public speaking with caution. Too
many of them take your money and leave you at the end of the
sessions with better phrases to describe what you still cannot do.
Others give you dated tricks ("Tell them what you're going to
tell them, tell it to them, and then tell them what you have told
them." Yawn, Yawn.) Others have an Ideal Public Speaker
stereotype and are in the business of turning out speaking
sausages.

Ultimately what you are seeking is not so much
communications training as transport education. One of the best
communications lecturers I know maintains that 9 out of 10
people are good communicators when they are under no
pressure. Most of us can be wise or funny or informative over a
dinner table or in a pub or on a golf course. Put us on a platform
in front of eight hundred people, or in a television studio before
an unseen audience of millions, and that wisdom, humour and
capacity to inform deserts us. We cannot TRANSPORT the
easy talker we are in unthreatening situations into a more
pressured context. So, if you are seeking to have your
performance improved by training, you need to find someone
who has the insight, the time and the competence to identify
your real life communications strengths and help you take them
with you into the public arena.

How Can I Sound Right?

Saying "you know?" at the end of every sentence is a very bad
habit. Right? Right? Emm, so is Aaah, you know what I mean?
Engaging your mouth before you engage your brain. These bad
habits are usually known to those who know and love or hate

you. Ask them about recurring phrases or vocal idiosyncras
they find irritating about you, and solve them well in advance of
your next public appearance. Make sure you have an ongoing
ally in this area. Habits continue to develop, so even if you sort
out the Right? Right? habit this year, by next year you may have
grown a quite different nasty. Make sure, if you have to make
many public appearances, that you have somebody listening
with a discriminating ear. And watching with a discriminating
eye. All of us develop odd grimaces or mouth clicks unknown to
ourselves which can be eliminated once we are aware of them.
(This is where public speaking classes using video are often
helpful, regardless of the competence of the tutor. You see
yourself and you learn how not to.)

Some time ago, I worked with a business speaker, who, at his
first rehearsal for an appearance answering questions on a
public platform, showed a tendency to say "actually" several
times in every paragraph, and under pressure, several times in
every sentence. The following week, when he returned, the
word had been eliminated.

"I offered everybody in the office and each member of my
family a tenner for every time they spotted me using the word,"
he told me, adding that the first two days had damn nearly
bankrupted him, but that it had not only eliminated his pet
irritant, it alerted the people in his office to their own.

Chapter 3

Preparing to Speak

> Great talkers are so constituted that they do not know their own thoughts until they hear them issuing from their mouths.
>
> *Thornton Wilder*

All of us deal, all day long, in speech. Yet, when it comes to preparing to speak in public, we tend to adopt all of the priorities of written presentation. We think in terms of introductions and expositions and summaries.

Hold it right there. The best spoken presentation, not surprisingly, follows the way we talk to each other. So that's how we need to prepare for speaking in public. We're not:

- Writing an essay
- Preparing a CV
- Creating a press release
- Developing a thesis

We're preparing to *speak*.

So we need to look at how people speak. We need to listen to the way they do it. The way they order their thoughts, attract attention, present their data. We need to pay attention to why we understand each other and how it comes about that we remember some things which are said to us, and fail to remember others.

Picture this. I am in bed, late on a Saturday morning, reading several books and uninterested in the wider world. The bedroom door opens and my eleven year old son is standing there.

"Hey," he says. (Enter speaking is his basic rule.)

"Mmm," I say. (He has now established that I am awake—an important prerequisite to communication with anybody. Don't believe what you have read about playing tapes to people who are asleep so that in ten days they understand ancient Greek. In ten days, all they understand is that a silent bedroom leads to a more pleasant sleep.)

"Sharks have such a high pain threshold," my son continues, "that in a feeding frenzy, one of them might have his tail bitten off by another and he won't even notice, he'll keep feeding. And if his own tail floats by him, he'll eat it, too." I gaze at him in silence.

"I don't suppose their tails do get bitten off a lot, though," he adds. "Sharks prefer to go for something that's already bleeding. You'd think a high pain threshold would be an advantage, wouldn't you? But it isn't in people. In humans, it's very dangerous. There's one little girl in California and she's all the time covered in bruises and burns. All over her hands is scarred." (At this point, by way of visual aids, he extends his own hands to me. They are very dirty, and I resolve to make him clean them.)

"This little girl in California doesn't feel pain. Her parents have an awful time trying to protect her because without a sense of pain, you have no natural sense of self-protection. So they have to try and do it from outside and they can't always figure out what she's going to do or what's going to endanger her. It must be awful. I mean, if you were this kid with the high pain threshold, your parents would be more like policemen than parents. Always telling you not to do things and you wouldn't be able to figure out why, because you never felt the pain from the accidents that happened to you, so there'd be no logic to what they were doing, they'd just be restricting you. They'd basically be pains in the ass. Although I suppose if they explained a lot as she got older, she'd eventually get the hang of what they were doing. Can I eat the rest of the cake from last night?''

The brief silence this non sequiter provoked he construed as consent, and was gone to assault the cake with dirty hands. That conversation—if you could call it a conversation, given my lack of audible participation—happened six months ago. Yet I can remember it in great detail and probably verbatim, because it was classically good spoken word communication:

1. The speaker had figured, rightly, that his mother would be interested in things to do with parents, kids and pain.

2. He got to the point. No introductions or self-justifications. No predictions as to what he planned to talk about. No promises as to how valuable I would find the information he was about to lay on me.

3. He painted the picture and then explained the concept out of it, not the reverse, which never works, but is the way most people prepare to speak in public.

4. He talked vividly. Sharks and blood and feeding frenzies and scars and policemen.

5. He stated, then qualified. Having made the point that the kid would think her parents were policemen, he then watered it down a bit. But he didn't do the reverse: dilute a reality he was only in the process of establishing.

6. He linked the thing well. Having made it clear that sharks had a high pain threshold, he then bridged into the wider concern, i.e. you would think this was a great advantage, but in human terms it is a major disadvantage.

7. He kept it short and kept irrelevancies out of it. I heard no details about the swimming speed of sharks or the lifestyle of

Californians.

8. He got on the next thing, rather than waffling on about the significance of what he had just told me.

Nothing special about it. Eleven year olds tend to communicate well, because the capacity has not been educated out of them by that age.

Those of us who are older have to prepare very carefully and precisely in order to achieve the same effect. If we devote enough time to the preparation, the delivery can be as effortlessly exciting. To facilitate such preparation, Carr Communications' Head of Training developed a deceptively simple Preparation Grid.

What points am I going to make?	How am I going to make them?	What are the obvious questions?	What are the nasty questions?

Let me show you how the grid can be used by referring back to the Saturday morning outburst by my son. Imagine, if you will, that a speaker takes as his topic *The Importance of Pain*. This speaker is addressing an audience of parents at a weekend designed to alert them to some of the problems of adolescence including drug-taking.

So the first point he wants to make is that there is such a thing as a pain threshold, and that it serves a protective function. Accordingly, he writes down in the first column the words you see in the illustration. The next point he wants to make is that humans have always sought to control pain. So down, as the second point in the same column, go the words *History of Pain Control*.

The speaker who wants to address the importance of pain plans to talk for twenty minutes, and take questions thereafter. In twenty minutes, he can hope to make somewhere between four and six points. More than that, and he is giving himself an unmanageable shopping list and providing his audience with something which, because it will be too fast and too detailed, will neither be readily understood nor easily remembered.

Our speaker decides that he would be better to make four points well, and if possible repeat some of them in different ways, than go for a higher number of points score. So he concludes that first column when he has listed his fourth point.

Now it is time for him to move into the column next door. This column is going to force him to work out how he can take the concepts he has outlined in column one and turn them into real live ideas which can be understood by people immediately, bearing in mind that they cannot take time out to revise a difficult point in a public gathering when he is in full spate. In addition to being immediately accessible, the material in the second column must be easy to recall.

What that means is that he must seek to give illustrations or examples in the second column. He must put feet under the notions in the first column. He must give concrete specifics instead of vague general statements.

So, in going back to the first point, he notes down the words *Sharks/Feeding Frenzy*. Under them go the words *California Child*.

Moving to the next point, he decides he needs to do some research. In this, he is unusually wise. Many public speakers deliver unstartling generalities which are not always factually correct. Long after the alligators in the sewers of Manhattan had been dismissed as urban legend, I heard it quoted as Gospel by someone making the point that children should not be given pets for Christmas because they tired of them so fast. After all, he said passionately, look at all those little pet alligators flushed down New York loos when their trendy toddler owners got tired of them...

Having done his research, the speaker is able to talk about herbs used in prehistory to control pain, about soldiers using alcohol and biting bullets during amputations, and about the discovery, towards the end of the last century, of aspirin and its first administration to a patient.

You can see what is happening. The concepts in the first column are becoming realities in the second column. If we are in the audience, we can see them, hear them, imagine them.

What he is achieving, in the process, is the development of a linked series of chunks of information. This is going to be crucially important to his performance, because under pressure of an audience, a straightforward list of apparently equally important informational elements is very difficult to remember and deliver in a interesting way.

Example. Someone calls out a series of digits to you.

8011353198977715

You just hear the sequence once, and then you're asked to recall them aloud. After three or four digits, on average, you're floundering. You may remember that somewhere in there were three sevens in a row, but precisely *where?*

Eventually, you peter to a halt, irritated with yourself because, dammit, you ought to be able to remember a few simple digits, right? Wrong. You are not a computer. You do not store information without reference to its significance.

Now, let me tell you why I can remember that particular sequence of numbers easily. Effortlessly. First thing in the morning. Last thing at night. Even if you spring it on me.

If you are working in the US, as I frequently am, then you want to ring home. So the first number you dial is 8011. That gets you onto the International Exchange of AT&T. 353 then directs your call to Ireland. 1, all on its own, gets you to Dublin.

(Within Ireland you have to put a nought before the 1 but on an international exchange, 1 on its own does fine.) 989777 is my company's telephone number. 15 is the extension where the Administrator hangs out.

We store information in chunks of significance. Public speakers must deliver data wrapped in its own significance. Facts should never be delivered in a vacuum. They must be packages so we understand them.

If a public speaker, for example, attacking the chemical industry, says that following the Bhopal disaster, Union Carbide made an immediate offer of one million dollars to the victims, most of us will register the figure without being pushed much one way or the other. But let the speaker tell us that 20,000 people died at Bhopal in the most excruciating and degrading agonies, that the survivors have suffered crippling and disabling illnesses, that Bhopal has had an unusually high level of eye disease and of stillbirth since the disaster— and, most important of all—that the one million dollars, divided among those damaged, amounts to no more than five dollars each. Then we know what we are meant to think. We have been offered the significance, wrapped around the chunk of data. We have been offered what we can envisage, understand and remember, rather than a sterile forgettable verbalised concept.

The second column, therefore, must provide a reality-testing exercise for the concepts in the first column.

It forces the speaker to develop the syringes which will allow the delivery of the material into the minds of the people listening. But, just as important, it provides the speaker with arguably the best way of remembering his own material. If this grid is used for preparation, and the speaker (having noted key words from the second column on a series of cards, one point per card) talks out each chunk of material several times, then the material will recur to him easily and fluently on his feet in front of an audience, prompted only by casual glances at the cards.

Rehearsing with cards is a skill all on its own. First of all, you must never assume that the normal size of notewriting will do. Put someone in front of a desk in their office and ask them to scribble a few little notes and they will do precisely that; *scribble* a few *little* notes. Put those notes in his hand in front of an audience of a thousand strangers and tell him to go for it, and a strange thing happens. He looks down at the cards and instead of clear words cueing his next thought, what he sees are little black worms crawling meaninglessly across the paper.

So, when you are making notes for later public use, make them in fat black felt tip pen and about twice as clear and big as you think is necessary.

Do not, having prepared your notes, then go in front of the mirror and orate. Mirrors are banned. You will not see yourself when you are performing in reality, so why should you develop the stage phoniness mirror-rehearsal invariably induces? Walk around your room or sit at your desk and talk. Do not try to remember the precise sequence of words that happened the last time. That is the route to the childhood disaster. You know the one? Where the child is asked to say a poem at the school concert, and dries up halfway through. Even if he is given the next words, the little girl cannot pick up; she has to go back to the beginning and start again, because what she knows is not an idea, but a rigid sequence of words. If you are going to articulate an idea to people in public, then you should never get into the position of having learned a rigid sequence of words. But let's be honest. It's very tempting. You say it aloud and, fortuitously, you hit a phrase that sings. Gosh, you think. Aren't I a witty little person, then? Aren't I fluent? Felicitous, even?

Except that, having got confident about that one phrase, you lose confidence in your capacity to ever *ex tempore* come out with anything comparable, and you try to wrap that sequence of words indelibly around that concept. The end result, sadly, is that you are not talking to people. You are repeating your private self in public. You are not giving the listeners a premiere; you are in replay mode.

When rehearsing with cards, shuffle them every now and again so that they come up in the wrong order. This is useful for two reasons. It challenges you to examine and re-examine the logic you have adopted in the original sequence. (Sometimes you find that you have inadvertently developed a better ordering of your material by shuffling the cards.) In addition, you learn to be able to talk out each chunk independently of what has gone before. Each has its own value. Each springs to your mind through a few key words on the card in your hand.

Never staple cards together, and never write on the back of them. Where possible, do not write full sentences. If you MUST write a complete speech—and there are occasions when this is inescapable—then turn to page 36 and find out how to do it. But don't crowd bits of a half-assed speech onto cards and kid yourself that they are just cue cards. They're cue cards the way roast turkey and two veg is a snack.

We left the grid a few pages back. But we have gone through the first two columns. The third column is another reality-tester. What would be the predictable questions your audience would like to ask? Think out the answers and make notes—either incorporate some of what you can infer as their concerns into your main speech, or have the material to hand to address them when it comes to the question-and-answer session.

The final column is the Stinkers. Our speaker is addressing a large group of concerned parents. Present also will be some teenagers. The parents basically want the kids scared to death of drugs and made them feel guilty in advance for their desire to experiment. The speaker knows they will ask questions designed to help him along that road.

One of the kids, though, may have a different agenda. One of the kids may decide he has had it up to here with teenagers always being portrayed as drug addicts when his father never draws a sober breath and his mother is permanently zonked on tranks. So he shoves the hands deep in the pockets, rises to his feet and speaks.

"Isn't it true that parents are much worse, statistically, as drug abusers than kids?" he asks. "Isn't it true that most kids that become drug addicts don't buy their first fix outside the school gate—they get it out of their mother's handbag?"

That's a stinker question.

If the speaker happens to represent a pharmaceutical

company, a stinker question may accuse the industry of having developed a culture in the "advanced" West which rejects pain and believes there is a magic bullet for everything. It does not matter what the stinker is, the speaker, long in advance of appearing on the platform, should have addressed the possibility of it being asked and mustered the material for a response, either incorporating it in the speech or readying it for the interactive session.

An industrialist recently walked into a stinker at an AGM. He was outlining a radical change in corporate direction, and seeking to enthuse the financial journalists present about the new market his business was going after. One of the journalists audibly boggled.

"With the kind of premises YOU have?" he half-asked, half-sneered, "You must be kidding."

The industrialist dithered and blustered. Afterwards, he admitted to his PR people that he—and they—could have predicted that a query might be raised about their dated and rundown branches.

"The truly annoying thing is that our figures for next year take into account a re-furbishing of those branches," he said.

"Why didn't you say that?" his PR people asked.

"Well, I remembered the figure, and then I thought 'but refurbishing admits that they're rundown, can I afford to admit that?' and then the journalist said something else snide that annoyed me and the really good answer didn't occur to me until two hours afterwards. I could have made a major positive point out of that negative query."

The French have a word for that. They call it *l' esprit de l' escalier*. Which means, roughly translated, that you come on up with the really crushing rejoinder, the marvellously scrumpling riposte, not during the argument, but as you're heading up the stairs for bed that night, when it's no good to you. That is why this book will stress again and again that prior to any public appearance, whether it be a speech or a TV interview you give privately, you should anticipate the worst possible thought which just might be in a listener's mind, so that if he decides to share it, it becomes an *ambiguous opportunity* rather than an unambiguous threat. (If more PR people thought along these lines, it would prevent them having to go public and declare their last statements or actions "inoperative" as Nixon's PR man had to do more than once. The most outrageous example of a corporate ignoring of the barely-hidden stinker happened in the year when most coverage was given to the drug Thalidomide which had so grievously distorted the bodies of thousands of children in Europe. Distillers, who in Britain and Ireland marketed the drug, sent bottles of their Johnny Walker Red to highprofile journalists that Christmas in the usual lets-butter-up-the-hacks exercise. One journalist promptly sent the bottle back and used his column in the Sunday newspaper three days later to excoriate the company and its damn nerve in assuming that a good image could be bought with cheap giveaway bottles while it was negotiating to save itself compensation money.)

When you have filled in the grid, go back, finally, to the first column. Does it start with the first point—the first real point you want to make, or have you developed introductionitis, a chronic disease of non-communicators who want to put everything in context before they tell you anything, who want to qualify everything rather than make interesting statements, who want to half-fill every bottle with cotton wool to frustrate your attempts to get to the actual contents of that bottle.

Remember the way eleven year olds operate. They are too young to have developed introductionitis. Instead, they go first to the most interesting thing they can think of. Would that more public speakers took lessons from them.

Every time you talk in public, you should prepare according to this grid. Every time is serious. Every time, you are talking to people who have not encountered you before, and who deserve better than to be tossed a half-remembered assortment of thrice chewed cud, dotted with oft-repeated shinies.

Content is more important than anything else. Later in this book, we will look at peripherals like clothing and make-up. But the single most important point about communication is that if the content of what is offered is relevant to the auditor, the appearance or vocal tone of the speaker becomes less important. Put it this way.

You walk into my office and tell me I have just won a quarter of a million in the Lottery. I don't much care if you have a dull tie on. In fact, if I was in bad enough financial disarray before you arrived with your announcement, I might not notice if that dull tie was ALL you had on.

Don't flatter yourself by too much personal vanity. Concentrate more than anything else on the delivery of relevant content in a way that is understandable and memorable and you will be surprised how quickly you develop a reputation as a good public speaker.

Dull tie and all...

Chapter 4

Writing for the Spoken Word

> He uses none but tall, opaque words, taken from the first row of the rubric, words with the greatest number of syllables, or Latin phrases with merely English terminations.
>
> *William Hazlitt on Dr Johnson*

If there were no good reasons for writing full length speeches, we could all live happily ever after, clutching bundles of white cards and being well-planned "naturals."

Sadly, there *are* some good reasons why full length scripted speeches are needed. They are needed where complex concepts have to be translated simultaneously. They are needed where a conference subsequently publishes the papers delivered on the day. They are needed where you are the scriptwriter, and somebody else is the speaker.

If you have to write a script for yourself or somebody else, then you must write it for delivery, first and foremost. So it is later going to be published in the book-of-the-conference? So that is a secondary objective. Your first objective is to write a fascinating speech that somebody can actually SPEAK. You can later edit and re-write the central points into something an uninitiated stranger can enjoy in print.

Writing a fascinating speech somebody can actually speak sounds dead easy, but it is one of the most difficult writing tasks anybody can take on. Many good writers cannot write dialogue. Good essayists, for starters find it very difficult to put first person language on the ideas they wish to explore. When direct speech is done well, it is easy to read and looks as if it was easy to write. It leaps off the page at you, because it feels like something you would say yourself. There's a marvellous line in *To Kill a Mockingbird*, for example, where the young narrator remarks that in her home, nobody ever ate chicken unless they were sick or the chicken was. That quotation became such currency in our family because we didn't much go for chicken that when a cousin of mine read the book, she was startled to find that Harper Lee had written the sentence. She thought we had. Many great books show the writer climbing inside the mind and thoughts and language of the narrator and sustaining the right words from beginning to end like *Huckleberry Finn*.

Once you are used to writing dialogue, it is very difficult to write any other way. When the Florida Society for the Book asked the late John D. MacDonald for an essay on the importance of reading, he slaved for eight fruitless months. He had the ideas. He had the data on the value of literature. But it wouldn't come out right. Eventually, one of the people at the Society suggested he might cast it as a conversation between his macho Floridian house-boat-dweller Travis Magee and his intellectual pal Meyer. Within days the conversation—all 8,000 words of it—had been written and was subsequently published. MacDonald, clearly, had developed a habit of thinking the way people speak. That is what you must develop if you have to write speeches for yourself or somebody else.

But then, MacDonald knew Travis Magee and Meyer. For more than twenty years, he had known them. Not to mention that he had, in the first place, invented both of them. If you are writing for someone else, then you have to know them, too. Last year, I was asked by an overseas client company to write a speech for one of their retiring executives.

"But I don't know the man," I said.

"Don't worry about it," they said comfortably.

"Keep it short. Keep it simple. Get him to make a few general comments about the corporation's history and a few nods toward the future, and it'll work."

I wrote the speech and Faxed it to them.

"Hey, this is great," their PR girl told me on the phone an hour later. "You won't be bothered if we take out the reference to the aviation book?"

"I know he won't have read that particular book," I said. "But I didn't feel that— "

"Oh, that's not the problem," she interrupted me cheerily. "It's not that he wouldn't have read that particular book. It's that he would never have read ANY book. Anytime. Any place. Everybody in the audience would know that, so if he made a reference to a book he had read, that would make them laugh, you know?"

Out came the reference to the book, and in went a reinforcement of a belief I have had for years which is that it is virtually impossible to write a good speech for someone unless you know the pattern of their speech and the habits of their mind.

Not so long ago, I was training a bright female executive, employed by a state agency, in speechwriting. She was going to have to write regularly for a major public figure. She had never met him. I told her she had to. She got in touch with his secretary and asked if she might attend an event at which he was speaking. The secretary asked why.

"I'm going to be writing for him, and I figure I should know what he looks like and sounds like and the way he thinks," my trainee said.

"In that case, you need to know more than you'll gain by seeing him on the platform," said his secretary. "Why don't you travel to the conference and back from the conference in his car and talk to him? Or perhaps I should say *listen* to him?

It was a great idea. One and a half hours to the conference, a half hour's speech at the conference, and a return journey of one and a half hours gave the new speechwriter material for months. The following day, she noted down just some of what she had learned about a man who, up to then, had been a name and a face in a newspaper picture:

He was gentle with machinery and could persuade even on-the-blink technology to work for him. Because he didn't believe other people were similarly gentle with machinery, he hated being asked to lend dictaphones and other gadgets.

He hated cigarette smoke.

He could remember every bit of poetry he had learned at school and college. Because he loved language, he could also quote bits from the Bible.

He loved gardening, was good at it, and had a particular affinity for the selection and propagation of trees.

He hated informality in clothing—to such an extent that he never took off his jacket or rolled up his sleeves. If you were at work, you should, he believed, be dressed for work, and you should invest in the best clothing you could afford.

He was a golfer and a competitive one.

He loved music, sang well and, unexpectedly, had a passion for singing Gregorian chant. His car cassettes concentrated heavily on traditional jazz going back to King Oliver.

He liked to read history, particularly social history, but read slowly. His last book had been on Egyptian building practices at the time of Ptolemy. Hated newspapers.

He had done oil painting in his youth, and a little sculpture, although this was not known and he did not want it to be known. He had a strong visual sense, and an obsession with architectural proportions.

He liked dogs as long as they were big dogs.

He could be very funny in his observations about people, but he never told jokes.

As you can see, by the end of that first encounter, my trainee had enough material to ensure that what she wrote for the man had a context and a flavour which were personal and authentic. In addition, because she had listened closely to the *way* he *talked* she knew which phrases would sit well in a speech for him, what were his sources of reference, how he behaved when he was working up to making a major point.

Watching him on the platform had taught her how he gestured, looked at an audience and built up to his concluding point.

That kind of research should always be done before you try to write for someone else. Once you know your man or woman, you can give them material that will sing. Once you know your man or woman, you can take risks for them and with them. Not so long ago, I had a client speaking directly after lunch in the middle of a conference where the contributions were going to be long and (I figured) extremely taxing on the listeners. My client was introducing the afternoon events, and was required to speak for only eight minutes. The assumption on the part of the organisers was twofold.

A. He wouldn't say anything of importance; all he had to do was arrive and be a visible VIP.

B. He wouldn't send them to sleep.

In fact, my client wanted to make a couple of important points and was terrified that, in the dead post-lunch hour, filled with good food and better claret, they would drift off. I took his points and gave him an introduction which suggested that they were all dying to go to sleep, and maybe even *deserved* a nap. But could they hang on for seven and a half minutes? They could? Well, in that case, any of them who had second hands on their watches could time him. Because he was going to take precisely seven and a half minutes. He then made his first point. Repeated it in different words—and announced that he had used up two of his minutes. There was a rueful laugh from those who had been timing him. He then made his next point, related it to the first, and glanced up.

"How'm I doing?" he asked.

As with one voice, they answered him.

"Two minutes left!"

He then made his last point, summarised what he had said without making it sound like a summary, and casually added "I figure I should stop right now, don't you?".

What neither I nor the speaker had anticipated was that several of the men present would have those watches which you can use as miniature alarm clocks, and, goaded by his initial promise, which they did not believe, they had set those alarms. As he finished, several of the watches tweeted, and the electronic comment on his timing brought the house down. It was a gamble that paid off, because they had been woken up enough to hear what he said and be amused by the way he said it.

You need to know your speaker awfully well before you can suggest a device like that to him, and he needs to trust you as a writer in order to go for it.

So, now let's deal with the basics of writing for the spoken word.

Put a pen in a speaker's hand, and it will tend to produce written, rather than spoken English. And there is a difference. We speak one way, and write another. We speak in short sentences; we write in subordinate clauses. We speak for immediate comprehension; we write for eventual comprehension. We speak with much more than words; we write with words alone, and often too many of them.

To write a script that will "talk" well entails having the courage to live with the fact that it may look less than perfect in print. Nicholas George, a one-time Director of Radio News for the BBC, in a reporters' briefing, laid considerable stress on this.

The best radio writing usually looks unbeautiful in print. We're not used to it. We speak one way and write another. What we would like you to do is to write the way most people speak. Most people speak in short sentences or half-sentences. The language is usually uncomplicated. When you write a radio report, the language has to be uncomplicated. The language must be plain. Sentence structure should be simple. Simple subject, simple predicate. No compound sentences.

The problem about putting this into practice is that we were all taught at school to seek, in essay writing, for a semi-academic tone of detached authority, and it is for that tone we unconsciously reach when we try to write a talk. The result would often look good in an up-market newspaper. Try to reduce it to short phrases on a card, however, and it rebels.

Translating the habit of "written" English into workable spoken English is a matter of breaking up the massy sentences, cutting out the posh civil service phrases, and structuring the thing so that it is actually possible to say it. One of the big causes of nerves among essay-readers is the awful knowledge that there is a chunk on the next page which consists of one main sentence and three subordinate clauses tied together with grammatical elegance in such a way that only someone with twice the normal lung capacity could possibly get through it on one breath. So either the speaker has to go through the whole lump of material at a wild trot, deteriorating into wheezy *sotto voce* towards the end, or pause inappropriately half-way through and suck in a breath which, it is hoped, the audience will not register.

The temptation to write written as opposed to spoken English is doubly strong if the speech has to be in some way vetted by someone Upstairs before you deliver it.

People Upstairs are notoriously inept when judging this kind of material. They usually do it in a judgemental and defensive frame of mind. Firstly, they have been put in the position of judges, or have put themselves in that position, so they feel demeaned if they find no fault in the speech, and secondly, they are much more interested in the internal accuracy of the document than its external reality and appeal. Secondly, they instinctively reject short sentences, colloquialisms, vivid examples and above all, repetition. People Upstairs want everything to take the form of elegant prose; the kind of prose you expect in the leading article of a newspaper or a good book. What they forget is that people reading a newspaper or a section of a book can stop at what they see as the obviously important places and re-read them. Or, the sub-editor may decide to help that process along by putting the vital material in a different typeface, to attract and hold the reader's interest. In radio, and from a platform, you cannot do that, short of (in platform speeches) turning your back on the audience entirely and writing the key points on a blackboard, which reduces the audience to resentful schoolchildren. So repetition is important. Not literal repetition. People will not hold still for a chorus of the same thoughts in the same words. But a recap, using different illustrations, will help the listener not to miss out on something which is significant.

So you resign yourself to the possibility of your script looking as simple and straightforward as it really is, shorn of all its prosy prose. Writing down the phrases you will actually say comfortably on your feet is a matter of talking aloud to yourself as you prepare, and being constantly vigilant. Talk aloud, Try out the various phrases, the various ways of making your points before you put them down on paper. You will also learn that some listeners do not hear continuous prose. They hear chunks of material and digest them into prose. So you need to talk in chunks and think your way from chunk to chunk.

The great master who is always worth listening to on this one is Alistair Cooke whose long-running *Letter from America* series on BBC Radio is a continuing tutorial for writers who need to produce speakable scripts.

Do not allow phrases to slip by you onto the page simply because you like the look of them. That in fact may be the key reason for their removal. Somerset Maugham said that all writers should go through everything they write and find the three things they most like in the text. Once identified, these three should be cut as arguably the most self indulgent. Dr Samuel Johnson had got there before Maugham.

"Read over your compositions," he told writers. "And, when you meet with a passage which you think is particularly fine, strike it out." Sir Arthur Quiller-Couch responded along similar lines to a novice's question.

"If you require a practical rule of me," he wrote, "I will present you with this: Whenever you feel an impulse to perpetrate a piece of exceptionally fine writing, obey it wholeheartedly and delete it before sending your manuscripts to press. *Murder your darlings.*"

Murdering your darlings is twice as important if you are generating them for the spoken word. It is three times as important if you are writing the spoken word for someone else to utter.

An example of this murdering process in action happened in my own business recently, when a managing director of one company within a massive multinational needed to make a speech to the collected international Chief Executive Officers (CEO) in London. It was an important presentation, and the man accordingly set aside plenty of time to prepare. He sent me background material ten days in advance and asked me to write a script for him. One week in advance of the presentation, he did his first read-through in our TV studio. The basic speech worked very well. There were a couple of quotations from Drucker and Tom Peters and other gurus that he liked a lot, and a few witty phrases. When we looked at the playback, one of the quotations came out, because it wasn't quite *him* and he said he needed to go away and get some extra facts and figures to beef up another part of the script.

Next day a few more personally important points went in, and a Drucker quotation came out. On the fourth day, Tom Peters fell by the wayside. On the fifth day, my witty phrases got the chop, because in commenting on what he was saying, he had come up with cracks which were more precisely geared to this audience, their perception of him, and his very individual, very understated style of delivery. When he delivered the speech in London, there were no remaining transplants. All had been replaced by his own words, his own thoughts. Worried that I might be hurt at the amputation of chunks of the original script, he kept pointing out how much he had liked it. However, the editing which had been done had made it more personal, more easy to read, more precise and shorter. He returned from his trip covered in encomiums and with several million quid in his back pocket to finance a major acquisition. Clearly, it had been a good speech delivered well.

So the watchword is cut. Cut again. The phrases you most like are probably those which owe most to the written word and have least to do with the spoken version. They coast in because there is a belief in the back of every speaker's mind that an audience is a mass, and therefore to be treated as inhuman. But at what point do people become an audience? When there are two people listening to you? Three? Three hundred? An audience is an agglomeration of individuals who will respond humanly if they are treated humanly.

The test is simple. You look at the phrase you have just written down, and ask yourself if you would say it in conversation to your best friend. If you would not, then it must come out no matter how you love it, because it will not earn its keep.

However, writing for the spoken word is not simply a matter of taking things out, cutting things down and reducing everything to a beautiful simplicity. On the contrary, it also requires more hard word from the speaker who is used to thinking and talking abstract concepts, because these simply do not work when speaking to an audience.

Have you ever watched a group in a lecture hall while some authority talked at length about some subject like rural depopulation? If, during that lecture, the speaker talked for a couple of minutes without creating some picture on which the minds of his listeners could fasten, then it must have been possible to hear the click of the button in people's minds marked "Off." People need pictures. From childhood onwards, key messages come to us in pictures.

Remember the second panel of our preparation grid given on page 27? In structuring what you want to write for yourself or another speaker, the material should be worked out and ordered according to the grid before you ever start to put words on paper. The second column of that grid, you will recall, was the one where you were challenged to produce specific examples to underpin general points, to paint pictures, to illustrate concepts, and to talk in vivid, real terms rather in abstract paragraph headings.

Accepting that people need pictures, it is still possible to write a book containing strings of abstractions, and, because it is in print, the book may succeed. The reader is in command of the situation. He can take all week to read the volume. Or all month. He can pause, to clothe the printed concept with his own illustrations.

Hand people over a woolly wordy concept from a platform, and you will lose them for three minutes while they try to reduce it to the picture you should have presented in the first place. An example from psychologist Robert Thouless—(*Straight and Crooked Thinking*):

Written concept

> The social value of instinct transformation is the fact that it can provide a socially harmless outlet for otherwise objectionable behaviour tendencies.

Pictorial example

> It is a good thing for Tommy to play football, because he is then less likely to make a nuisance of himself by fighting other boys.

Thouless calls the mental task involved in producing example 2 instead of example 1, "challenging ourselves to give particular examples of illustrations of general statements."

Quite apart from the vividness of the pictorial statement and the much greater likelihood of it being remembered (take for example, Churchill's "An Iron Curtain has come down over Europe") the chances are that the apt pictorial illustration will be simpler and quicker to say than the general statement. It is easier to say "Hungry people aren't interested in writing poetry," than it is to say "deprivation of the nutritive instinct is destructive of the higher cultural interests." And people will understand it. And remember it. Perhaps even be moved by it.

There is nothing condescending about writing for the spoken word. If you have something to say which you believe to be important, then the best way to help people understand it is the way you should use. For most speakers, written, conceptual, non-visual speech is a trap into which they have been led by education, environment or their own feeling for the grandiose. Vaguely, they believe that certain phrases will, or should impress the public. They may have attended so many company or committee meetings that they now actually think in terms like "the advancement of the social structure." I heard one trade unionist in a recent radio interview, saying, apropos a certain factory, that "it carries a female labour quotient." I think he meant that it employed women.

Sometimes, of course, there is a concealed determination not to communicate. The speaker agrees to talk, or be interviewed, but has picked on a kind of language which effectively rules out the chances of most of the hearers understanding the talk. The following I once recorded when a British credit union organiser was talking on radio about their rules.

"There is corporate responsibility in regard to the allocation of mutually subscribed funds to individuals. This entails an enquiry into the objects for which the disbursement is required. If it is considered to be of a productive nature, then the committee will be free to release to the applicant some for the available capital. This would ensure that personal considerations on the part of the party allocating the funds will be negatived, and the aspect of mutual responsibility, which is a central part of the organisation's philosophy, will be stressed."

This may have made a great deal of sense to this man and his fellow committee members. It may also make sense to readers of this book who have time at their disposal to digest it. Translated into something which would have been interesting for people listening, however, it would need to run along these lines

"It works this way. You as a member, come along and ask for a loan. The committee decides if it's a good idea that we should give it to you. We'll ask you a couple of questions to find out if what you want the money for is 'productive'. That really means that if you just want to throw a big party, we'd think twice, but if you wanted a scooter to go to work on, we'd probably give you the money. We think it's better to have a committee because if there were only one person making this decision, then members would be able to complain that they'd been unfairly treated, and anyway, we think it's good for people to realise that a few other people care about them, and that by joining, they're caring, indirectly, for other people."

The translation isn't baby talk. In fact, it takes more time and is quite difficult to work out in advance, but the returns make it worthwhile.

A concern for making this visually appealing to people should not stop at talking about Tommy playing football as opposed to slinging stones at other boys. All of the tools of your argument should be made as interesting and accessible as possible to the listener. Take statistics. To talk about 1.3 people travelling to work in a car is just about acceptable in a newspaper. It is not acceptable at all in the spoken word, and will create an awful undercurrent of stifled laughter. Statistics should be worked so that the illustration carries roughly the same message as the bare figures. And where the bare figures are necessary, reduce them to understandable forms—talk about one person out of ten, instead of ten percent.

There are three main factors in selling people on an idea. The first is getting their attention so that they will listen. The second is making sure they understand it. The third is ensuring they remember it. Good writing for the spoken word does all three.

There are all sorts of ways to grab attention. There is a lovely example in the film Easter Parade where Fred Astaire is trying to assess whether or not Judy Garland, as a potential dancing partner, had "It." He told her that he would walk behind her on a crowded street, and if people turned to look at her he would then be sure she had "It." Followed a sequence where Judy Garland, positive she lacked "It," but hungry for the job, walked the length of the street in front of Astaire with her tongue stuck out further than seemed physically possible. People turned to gape. Astaire employed her.

When you are writing a speech, it is important to start in gear. To many speakers rev for several minutes in neutral before they get into first gear and take to the road. There is nothing more boring than watching somebody revving a static vehicle, and it ain't so good for the vehicle, either, especially if the person behind the wheel, conscious of the lack of progress, begins to roar the immobile engine. Heat. Noise. Exhaust. No progress.

Get into first gear quickly. Get rid of the revs. Revs like thanking the organisers for inviting you to this prestigious event, held for the eighth successive year in the No Hoper Hotel, Notown. Now, let's be clear. There is a lot to be said for making some personal observation which expresses genuine interest in the people or in their organisation. But it cannot be a dismissable ritual that they have heard before.

Remember the Hawthorne effect? Part of work-study apocrypha at this point, the roots of the story go back to the 'thirties in the US, when General Electric decided to have work practices at its plant in a place called Hawthorne studied to see what would improve productivity. The oddity which emerged was that contradictory factors seemed to have similar payoff. Up the lighting in one area, and productivity went up. Lower the lighting in another area, and productivity in that area rose, too. Eventually, the penny dropped. Wherever the workforce felt that attention was being paid to them and the way they did their work and the opinions they had, productivity went up, because they felt better about the whole deal. Every speaker—and everybody who writes for a speaker—should keep the Hawthorne effect in mind.

But the reference which is made to the listeners, or to an individual within the listening group, should not be stale or imprecisely reverential. It should be fresh, slanted, unexpected, funny or thought-provoking.

Another of my pet hates in the way of revs is when a speaker stands up and ploughs his way through everything the audience has heard the previous day, or worse still, everything they are DUE to hear later that same day.

"I note," the speaker says pompously, "that the eminent Professor Joe Bloggs has covered the question of affluence in the middle years of the private sector and has, in the process, addressed the oft-expressed concern of those in the blah blah."

People who write for politicians tend to have what could be called reflex revs. They give them two pages of historic boasts which evoke mutually competitive responses of boredom and irritation in the audience. Who the hell wants to know that when you came to office you implemented the third paragraph of the forty-first subsection of the internal directive on the care and fostering of wastepaper baskets?

All of which will lead some readers to the assumption that you should start with a joke. Oh no. Oh dear. Oh help.

They sell every year. They sell better than books about sex. The joke books. The Opening Anecdote books. The books which will give you three witty (that's their claim, don't make any judgements other than negative ones) openings on profits or losses or sales or exports. I have seen solemn men stand up and tell an opening joke and look as sadly silly as overweight sober CEOs slumming it at the staff Christmas party with paper hats on. I have seen frightened women get to the podium and walk leadenly through something once called a joke before it died. Women telling opening jokes are even worse than men telling opening jokes, if that is possible, because so few women are natural joke-tellers.

Let's get it on the record here and now. Whoever suggested that jokes were the infallible way to start a speech ranks up there along with Attila the Hun and Hitler as a killer. Whoever that person was has killed audiences by the gross and murdered potential speakers by the thousand.

By all means, read funny writers. Peter de Vries, P.G. Woodhouse, Robert Benchley, Stephen Leacock.

They may spark a funny thought. But do not start with the predictable bought-in joke. Please? Pretty please?

Where you start is by answering the unspoken question of the audience, which is usually general. It's likely to be one of these or a variant on them.

- What's the story?

- What's on your mind?

- What's new?

- Where do we go from here?

- What's bugging you? (Or, more chirpily, What's up, Doc?)

- What's cooking?

- What do you know that we should know but don't?

Your speech should start by answering one of those questions in the most vivid, lively, personal way possible. No jokes. None of those off-the-peg opening gambits you can buy in Public Speaking Guides. All those dreary debater's cracks like "using his argument as a drunk uses a lampost, more for support than illumination".

They are clichés, and a cliché says to its listener, "Mate, this is a road you've travelled before, so relax and put your mind in cold store for a while." Thumbing through a *Dictionary of Clichés* is chastening. So much of what we believe is freshly coined personal material is in fact old hat, like the phrase "old hat!"

What the public speaker is always aiming for is the cliché-free clarity and freshness of children's speech. You hear a child use an expression like "A barefoot head", and baldness takes on a new meaning.

Playing word games does help to both sensitise one to clichés in one's own usage of words, and to enliven one's speech. One such is the group name game. You know about a "pride of lions". Did you know about a "cooing" of doves, or a "gossip" of sparrows?

Irish raconteur Ted Bonner once quoted a series of these to a Canadian broadcaster in the course of a television programme. He was recalling the encounter of a group of nineteenth century English writers, among them Belloc, Chesterton, and HG

Wells, with what Belloc crudely called a "crowd of prostitutes." One of the quartet suggested that as writers, they ought to be able to coin a better collective term than that. After a moment, Chesterton offered "a jam of tarts," and was followed by Wells with "an anthology of English prose." Mr Bonner mentioned to the Canadian that he had spent months vainly trying to think of another on the same lines. The compere, in a moment of inspiration, suggested a novel of Trollope's. Apart from being fun, this sort of exercise is good for making one alert to the relationships between words and situations.

Use first degree words

These are the words which immediately bring an image to mind. Others must be "translated" through the first degree words before you see the image. Those are second/third degree words. First degree words are usually more precise, too.

First Degree Words	Second or Third Degree
face	visage, countenance
book	volume, tome
stay	abide, remain, reside

Anybody who speechwrites regularly or for a living should have an extensive library (see bibliography, page 182). *Fowler's Modern English Usage* must be an essential part of that library, as should his *The King's English* from which the following (not specifically related to speechwriting although vitally important to that craft) is taken:

> Anyone who wishes to become a good writer should endeavour, before he allows himself to be tempted by the more showy qualities, to be direct, simple, brief, vigorous and lucid. This general principle may be translated into practical rules in the domain of vocabulary as follows:
> Prefer the familiar word to the far-fetched.
> Prefer the concrete word to the abstract.
> Prefer the single word to the circumlocution.
> Prefer the short word to the long.

Prefer the Saxon word to the Romance.
These rules are given roughly in order of merit; the least is also the last."

Quiller Couch added a preference, in his Cambridge lectures *On Writing*, for transitive verbs.

"Generally use transitive verbs, that strike their object", said QC, "and use them in the active voice, eschewing the stationary passive, with its little auxiliary *is's* and *was's*, and its participles getting into the light of your adjectives, which should be few."

Making active verbs out of passives is a skill of writing—and of re-writing. Go back over your first draft, and if you find something like this:
"The military headquarters was occupied by insurgents," change it to
"Insurgents occupied the military headquarters."
Where possible use simple, vivid verbs:
"He *shoved* that thought to one side."
"She *sliced* through the waffle."
"He may not *pound* the table, but he emphasises..."
Avoid the whiches. Go back over your script, cut them out. Never mind that they are grammatically defensible (and I could argue with that one, too, if I had the time, which I do not). They are not defensible in spoken word terms. Nobody says to his mother at the breakfast table,
"The egg which I am eating has a possibility of being infected with salmonella."
If he does, the answer is,
"The feeling which I am having is that you should get out of here before I lose patience, which I am rapidly doing."
- The egg he's eating.
- The feeling she has.
- The possibility she may lose patience, because that's precisely what's happening to her and it's happening fast...

Where possible, in addition to being active and organising your own which hunt, get terse. Instead of this:

"The coming years are likely to see a signal decrease in the national requirement for smoke-producing solid fuels."

Try this:

"Coal has had it."

Get rid of padded nothings from your script. Here's a few I've picked at random from scripts I have edited in the last couple of months together with the simpler phrases or words substituted.

Padded Nothings	Substitutes
Factual information	Facts
At the present time	Right now
Short in length	Short
In the event of	If
It is quite possible that it looks like a fairly satisfactory level of consensus can be achieved.	We'll agree
An employee incapacitated in the performance of his duties by the onset of viral influenza.	A guy with flu, too sick to work.
In the majority of instances	Usually
On the grounds that	Because
Prior to	Before
In compliance with your request	As you asked
The aforementioned items	These (items)

This is to inform you that in due course, there will be an issue, to the relevant persons applying, of the appropriate...	We'll be sending this to the people who asked for it.

At all times, use contractions rather than full structures. Don't, shouldn't, can't, didn't, not, do not, should not, cannot, etc. Except where the full phrase will add emphasis or slow the pace and you have decided you want that effect. The old rule KISS (Keep It Simple, Stupid) applies to all writing for the spoken word. Some speechwriters resent this. Damn it all, they say, audiences should pay attention. This may well be true, but don't hold your breath. And don't project any duty on to the audience. Your speaker is the Responsible Voice. If he is boring, it's his fault. Not the audience's fault for finding him boring.

Nor does simplicity mean robbing material of its value. It sometimes kicks the material into life. A good example is quoted by Lilyan Wilder, President Bush's speech coach, in her book *Professionally Speaking:*

> Simplicity has power. One prominent Philadelphia lawyer made himself a fortune by putting this axiom into practice. At the turn of the century, people were suing railroad companies for deaths and injuries incurred at railroad crossings. The Pennsylvania Railroad Company hired the lawyer to write a legal notice that would tell pedestrians what their responsibilities were in averting accidents. His fee was $10,000—a lot of money, especially in those days, but a small price to pay for stemming the tide of liability suits. The company may have had second thoughts when they received the lawyer's notice. It was four words long: 'Stop, Look and Listen.'
>
> Yet these four words branded themselves on the mind of every American as no erudite dissertation could have done. Pedestrians became aware of their responsibilities. The accident rate at crossings fell. The tide of suits evaporated overnight.

Simplicity means more than simply picking first degree words and damping down your desire to show off—"Hey, Ma, look, I used the word peristalsis, so there,"—it also means shortening your sentences. Get launched, with pen in hand, on a good complex sentence, and you could still be going several minutes later. Examine the leading article (editorial) in any of the classier newspapers and you will find vastly complicated sentences which wander, without let or hindrance, through clause and sub-clause, in an out of brackets and subsidiary thoughts, until they mate up with a full stop. The newspaper in front of me has one sentence that goes on for 56 well-chosen words. It is readable, it is not sayable.

This does not mean that you have to talk in telegram language. It just means chopping up your sentences and varying their length to give some variety of pace. As Churchill did:

"Hitler said that as things develop he's going to wring England's neck like a chicken. Some chicken. Some neck."

The second thing Churchill did in that tiny extract was obey another of the cardinal rules of speechwriting. You must always state, then qualify.

"All crows are black," you say, and then you may add. "Although like humans, it is possible to have albino crows. Completely white ones. But they're rare. Very rare."

NOT

"Given the fact that, in common with many other animal and bird species, including human, there is the possibility of an albino bird in the crow species, nevertheless, all crows are black."

In making statements or raising ideas for an audience to consider, never insult them by rubbing their noses in their own ignorance, but never assume they know the full story. Find a way of explaining without sending up a flag that reads EXPLANATION.

One of the best ways of doing this is by rediscovering how you came to the knowledge you are now passing on, and re-living your excitement as somebody told you about this new software or that new method of oil extraction by the addition of molasses. Confess ignorance or recently-corrected ignorance. No? Why not? Better than you have! Witness:

Charles Lamb

My reading has been lamentably desultory and immethodical ...in everything that relates to science. I am a whole encyclopedia behind the rest of the world... I know less geography than a schoolboy of six week's standing...I am a stranger to the shapes and texture of the commonest trees, herbs, flowers...and am no less at a loss among purely town-objects, tools engines and mechanic processes.

Robert Benchley

I am never upset when I find that I know nothing about some given subject, because I am never surprised. I am familiar with several kinds of birds and flowers by sight, and could, if cornered, designate a carnation or a robin as such. But beyond that I just let the whole thing slide...

J.B. Priestley

I have no knowledge whatever of the sciences in which I once received a thorough if rudimentary instruction. My piano playing is gone; I cannot dance now or play football; my billiards and chess are contemptible; I could draw a little once, but that too has gone; even my French is vile, and I puff and pant, grow fat, and creep about in the shadow of a liver.

Ignorance is its own best protection, not only when sharing some information with an audience which may have a patchy prior knowledge of the data, but also when coping with questions from an audience following a speech. If you're asked a question to which you do not know the answer, you can *say* you don't know, or you can prove it. When in doubt, confess ignorance and express the desire to have it remedied.

Of course, every now and again you find an audience that doesn't know what you're talking about and doesn't really want the explanation, either. I found this in one individual plumber years ago, when I commissioned him to redo my bathroom and include in it a shiny new bidet. He had not encountered a bidet before, and pronounced it Budee, which gave it a regal Indian twang I had not anticipated.

"What's it for?" he asked, the day it was delivered.

I told him, and I thought I was going to have to have him resuscitated by a paramedic, he laughed so much.

"God, he wheezed," wandering away. "God, that's only great."

Next day, over a cup of tea, he asked me again. I told him again. Hilarity ensued again. Eventually he got his breath back.

"Jesus," he said, "you're a terrible woman. You really are. You're a desperate woman. Tell us what it's *really* for, though?"

Eventually, I gave in and told him it was for soaking tights.

"Ah, yes," he said, appeased. "Ahh, that'd make sense, all right."

Frequently when you are trying to introduce a new idea or explain a new concept, numbers or statistics come to hand. They should be managed with great caution. Most people sitting in an audience have very limited numeracy. If they do not have the figures in front of them on a piece of paper, a screen, or a calculator, they take on board the first set of digits you mention, then they take on board the second set, but by the time you get to the third set, the first set have rolled up out of their mind's eye view. Keep figures to a minimum.

Where you have to use them, reduce them to the lowest common denominator. Explain what a billion is. Talk about one in ten, not ten percent. Do not expect the statistics to explain themselves. If you do not know, for example, what the range of human temperatures is, then when someone announces that she had one of 103 degrees, you don't know whether to be glad or sorry for her.

Never take the human factor out of human figures. Stalin said that 30,000 men killed in a war was a statistic but that one child drowned in a pool was a tragedy.

There is always an instinct, when delineating a general truth, to talk in generalities. That's not how people come to terms with truths. Talk in specifics. Tell an individual story, made more individual by the detail you use in telling it, and out of that individual story, all of the people present will extrapolate the general truth. Remember Aesop's ables? In theory, he shouldn't have told them. I mean, he was trying to get people to understand general truths about daily lives, wasn't he? Except that he told simple specific anecdotes about individual animals and out of that, generations of people have learned varieties of things applicable to their own lives. It's true of all the great stories, whether from Greek mythology, the Bible or a modern novel; the more memorably individual and specific is the example, the more generally applicable is the truth which can be drawn from it.

That applies, too, to the ownership of the material. No speaker in public should be peddling general statements he or she does not own. Somebody once said that most lectures were a transference of bones from one graveyard to another. Public speeches should not be like that. You must not write a script which transfers data from an authority to an audience without running it through your speaker.

Nor should your speaker utter that speech without taking ownership of particular points—which is why speakers must always have time with a script in advance of delivering it. Sight-reading is a disaster, often excused by bright overworked people who know they can read a script on their feet and get away with it, and who assume too much responsibility on the part of the writer. There is a legend about an American President (the legend is never quite sure which one) who had a fight with his scriptwriter, but nevertheless went out later that day, live in front of an audience, script in hand. By page ten, things were getting exciting. He had outlined all of the major threats and challenges facing the nation. The last line on page ten said:

"Now, let me tell you how I'm going to tackle those threats."

He turned the page, and (again, according to legend) the only line on the next page was:

"You're on your own Buster!"

It may or may not be true. What is certainly true are two incidents that happened while I watched. In one, a businessman who was a survivor rather than a great brain stood up and read one page twice, because it had been photocopied twice. He didn't notice. We, listening, did.

The other occasion was when a pal was presenting an awards programme on television and a political leader read an address in the middle of it. There were four scripted pages. He handled it beautifully. Or rather, he handled the first three pages beautifully. When he turned to page four, it threw him just a little because it was blank.

Again, the person collating the thing, under pressure, had dropped in a white page instead of the real fourth page. The speechmaker turned whiter than the page in front of him and was rescued by the compere, who could see what had happened.

The moral? If you are the speechreader, *never, ever* read on sight. No matter what the pressures. If you are the speechwriter, insist that your reader has the time to read and if necessary amend your material. Otherwise you get blamed later.

One of the things you can get blamed for is introducing an unintended *double entendre*. Get someone else—someone with a young dirty mind to read your speech before it goes public. I speak from bitter experience, having used a couple of words which had more than one meaning in contexts where the second and more inappropriate meaning was likely to be the one picked up on. But then, as a radio interviewer, I did one of the dirtiest interviews ever, unintentionally, when asking questions of the organist belonging to a particularly historic church.

He had come into the studio to talk about a restoration fund for the organ, and my slip was to refer to it, continually throughout the interview, as his organ. So I asked him how dilapidated his organ was, and whether it was capable of the many variations as it used to be, and when people came into the Church were they allowed to handle his organ, or just gaze at it in awe. Halfway through the interview, the co-presenter got up and left the studio, which should have alerted me to the possibility that something was mildly wrong. Luckily, I found the man and his organ so fascinating that it never occurred to me to look into the control box, where I heard later, people from the highways and byways of radio had been dragged in and were lying around in states of collapse.

So, in addition to keeping your speechwriting simple and vivid, it helps if you keep it clean.

Never bend over backwards to use current slang in order to show how cool you are, or how cool is the speaker for whom you are writing. If you are in your twenties or older, then by the time you actually hear a 'new' word, it probably is no longer new.

In writing a speech, whether for yourself or for somebody else, you must always in speaking about societal groups, refer to them using the expressions they use to refer to themselves. Do not call travelling people tinkers or itinerants. Call them travellers. Do not call people queer or bent or homosexual if they prefer to be called gay. Do not call people negroes if they prefer to be called blacks. And do not call women either ladies or girls. The latter is acceptable in reference to under-seventeens, the rest are women.

One of the final checks you should do, when you have the material drafted, is check that it follows logically. Better still, that it follows *inescapably*.

At an actor's master class, I once heard a student ask the famous actor what was the trick to his superb timing. The actor, who is a practical performer rather than a theoretician, looked hunted for a moment. Then he smiled.

"I'll tell you," he said. "I never say a line until I can't NOT say the line."

It's much the same with a good speech. It should be so tightly linked that the progression to the next thought or idea is inevitable. This makes it easier to read, easier to deliver, easier to be confident about. It also makes it more understandable and memorable for the listening audience.

You know that you don't have good links either because they creak— "And having said we couldn't see the wood for the trees, let me move on to another kind of wood—the veneer of public relations…" Or because you find your script has suffered an outburst of the rhetoricals. The rhetoricals come about when the speechwriter crashes from one thought to the following thought by asking questions.

"And having dealt with poor internal communications, we have to ask ourselves, what about our public relations? How well are we doing there?"

I have heard speeches where every link was a rhetorical question. Not only is it lazy, but it invites the perverse and wrong answer from the audience, and even if the audience are too collectively polite to vocalise it, they will, individually, think bad thoughts.

My husband always reacts to the rhetorical question in the TV ad which asks:

"Tense, nervous headache?"

by snarling

"NO, I've got a lovely relaxed, integrated headache, thanks." Rhetorical questions stimulate natural human perversity and, as a result, tend to serve as a distraction. Using one just about once, in a speech, is acceptable, if the use of the form makes a point more dramatic. Litanies of rhetorical questions should never be used.

When a speech is finished, the speaker should become very familiar with it, but not learn it off by heart. In presenting a speech to somebody else, make sure it is double spaced, has great big margins, big white spaces at the top and bottom of the pages; the speechmaker, particularly if he is in a context with more than one speaker, needs places where he can add minor points or personal illustrations. Never try to economise on space. For a reader to glance down and see two dense paragraphs in front of him, asking to be ploughed through, amounts to an unfair pressure. When the speaker glances down, the speech should almost *read itself to him*. Like this:

"Today's awards are important.

Not because they're for effort.

Not because they're for achievement.

They're important because this is the first time any nation has halted a national direction because of the efforts of individuals who didn't protest, didn't write letters to the papers. Individuals who just did things the right way. And hoped the rest of us were looking.

Fortunately, we *were* looking..."

There are a number of oversized typefaces (Orator is the name of one of them) which can be used to make speech-reading a little easier. Be sure to check with your speaker, however, that he actually prefers an oversized typestyle. Some speakers prefer to see normal typing and some like their speeches typed in normal capitals. (I find this unreadable and have the instinct to shout the entire speech, but different strokes for different folks...)

Even if your speaker prefers the material in a normal typeface, do not release it to either press or audience beforehand. They will sit there, reading it faster than he can say it and discussing page 12 with the person sitting next to them. Release it only after it has been delivered. Don't release it at all if you can use a press release.

The last thing to do (and it is a lot easier to do it if you have the speech on a word processor, rather than a straight typewriter) is to do a fast which-and-cliché hunt. The whiches creep in at every rewrite. The clichés breed between words. You know them. Last, but not least. On my right, your left. So-and-so and his lovely wife Twiddles.

Excise them. Amputate them. Smother and replace them.

And remember, you can create your own clichés by using a favourite phrase or line too often. The first time I became aware of this was when I watched a speaker of charm, charisma, wisdom and humour attack a potentially boring subject with such zest that all of the audience wanted to sign up for a lifelong tutorial. Coming to the end of the talk, the speaker shoved his notes in his pocket.

"Do you know, the best advice anybody can give you is on the lid of a pot of jam," he told the audience. "You know what it says—it says 'pierce with a pin, and then push off.' I feel that's what I've done to my subject today—pierced it with a pin. Now it's time to push off. Thank you."

And off he went.

About two months later, I saw the same speaker handling a quite different subject in front of a radically different audience. Again, he made them laugh, made them think, challenged their prejudices and told them some truths. At the end he got the same response to his line about the lid of the jampot. He drove me home afterwards, talking about the evening.

"I don't think you should ever use the line about the jampot again," I said.

"Oh? did it not work?"

"It worked beautifully. But I'd seen it before, heard it before. There is always the chance that there is somebody in an audience who's seen you in action on another occasion, and it damages their sense of discovery if they hear you saying the same thing. Anyway, it's a lazy public speaker's device and you're too good to ever rely on something that worked on a previous occasion. You can create something new every time."

"You know something?" he asked thoughtfully. "You could get to be an awful pain in the ass."

Reader, I married him. And in the ensuing decade and a half, the jampot, to my knowledge, has never raised its ugly lid again. Unless he's doing it on the sly.

To sum up, then, in writing a speech you must do it in the spoken word, because people cannot revise or re-cap. They cannot research for your meaning on the spot—or if they do, you have lost their attention for the next point you wanted to make. So the stress is on:

Clarity

Simplicity

Pictures, not abstracts

Creative repetition of internal ideas

Removing clichés.

One final thought. Jargon has to be removed. No internal phrases. No corporate speak in public please.

What seems to you a simple and obvious way of talking about your subject may in fact be imported straight from the shop floor and so be virtually incomprehensible to others. It is good manners to make the effort to rejig what is axiomatic to you, so that it becomes interesting and understandable to others.

Jargon includes the neat dead phrases of internal memos, proposals to the management and justification for projects that fell on their noses.

Example

Is it a probability or, on the contrary, an unlikely outcome? Whether the former or tho latter be preferable would seem to admit of some difference of opinion; the answer in the present case being in the affirmative or the negative according as to whether one elects on the one hand to psychologically internalise the disfavour of fortuitous events, albeit in an extreme degree, or boldly envisage in adverse conditions the inbuilt prospect of bringing them to an advantageous eventual conclusion...

That is Hamlet's 'To be or not to be' soliloquy, jargonised. Awful, isn't it?

Chapter 5

Being at Ease, Looking at Ease

Nerves

> Great ideas, it has been said, come into the world as gently
> as doves. Perhaps, then, if we listen attentively, we shall
> hear, amid the uproar of empire and nations, a faint flutter
> of wings, the gentle stirring of life and hope.
>
> *Camus*

They were bright. Well informed. Authoritative. Each facing a
major communications challenge. Each, theoretically, just about
ready for it. Each ready to run for the hills, if they could just
decide which hill was nearest.

They didn't know each other. Nor will they.

The first was a man built like the stereotypical ambassador.
Grey hair—early grey, because he was in his late thirties. Solid
build, broad forehead, bright blue eyes, strong graceful hands.
This description was given to me in advance by his Personal
Assistant.

"Why do I need all this?" I asked. "Dammit, you just want me
to help this guy polish up a speech you've already written for him.
I don't need to know what colour hair his grandmother had."

"I'm telling you because this man looks as if he knows what
he's doing," the Personal Assistant said.

"I presume he does. He's unlikely to have got to be CEO in a
company your size if he *doesn't* know what he's doing."

"Right. Except when he stands up in front of an audience, it all
goes away. He goes catatonic. He thinks he's going to die. The
audience thinks he is going to die."

"So why does he put himself through this?"

66

"He has to. We're a multinational. He'll probably end up as V.P. somewhere if he shows he can communicate. Or even President of the Corporation. If he hides, he won't even be left where he is—it's just not that kind of company."

The unwilling communicator—startlingly named Frank—turned up later that afternoon, script in hand. I thought him uncivil because he barely greeted me and was evidently impatient to get on with it. We put him at the podium in studio, the technician had just enough time to take a voice test and he was off and running.

The first three pages were fine, if a touch fast and more than a little essay-ish in tone. Top of the fourth page he swallowed. Unsuccessfully. It is one of life's truly awful sensations when you begin a swallow and your throat seems to have forgotten the second part of the instructions. He stood there, strangling and gazing at his script in horror. I said nothing. My technician, Gerard, said nothing; but then, that's what he usually says.

"I knew this would happen," Frank said miserably.

I looked at him.

"The thing is, I used to take Valium when I had to talk but then there was all the stuff about addiction and I got scared. Anyway, my wife said it made me talk like an astronaut walks on the moon."

I laughed. He seemed surprised.

"My doctor's willing to give me Beta Blockers," he offered apparently willing to take whatever I offered by way of a second medical opinion.

"Before you get to that, explain the point you were making," I suggested. "I'm not very good with figures, and I didn't follow how the first half of the year could be so bad and then the second pick up so well. How could that be?"

He told me. He told me in vivid, simple, understandable terms. He looked at me. He waited until he was sure I understood one point before he went on to the next. When he couldn't remember the precise figures he was looking for, he recalled that they were on page 11 of his script.

"Hang on just a second," he told me. "This is worth getting

right. It shows a very interesting trend."

For a couple of seconds, he fished through the pages and came up with the figures. Having quoted them directly from the paper, he then expanded on their significance.

"But you're talking on Saturday to people in businesses quite different from your own," I reminded him. "Why should they care?"

On this, he got quite passionate. He had relaxed against the podium. Now he stood up and told me, counting off the three essential considerations on his elegant fingers, precisely why they should care.

I thanked him, and he immediately slipped out of transmission mode and back into panic mode.

"I knew it would happen," he muttered miserably, referring back to his "dry". "I just *knew* it would."

At this stage, the technician finally stopped video-recording, which he had continued to do during the "dry" and the subsequent conversation.

"The pickup point?" Gerard asked tersely (he has two gears; silent and terse. It makes him very restful company.)

I nodded. Frank, now miserable and confused in equal parts, sat down in front of the TV monitor.

"I want you to watch this man," I told him. "because this is the man you have to be on Saturday. This man knows his stuff. He cares about his audience. He's not self absorbed. He handles his scripted material as it should be handled; he owns it. It doesn't own him."

Frank at this point had decided we had some superb speaker on a standard tape that we wanted to show him to make him feel even more inadequate, and when his own face popped on to the screen, he was startled. The playback started just after his "dry," when he began to explain things to me. Except that because I was sitting in the front row of the audience seats, and because I had only asked perhaps three questions, the impression was of a man ad-libbing a prepared speech and doing it superbly. He goggled at how well he was doing. When we came to the end, I hit the OFF button.

"I know what you're going to say," I told him.

"You're going to say but"

He nodded.

"No *but*," I said. "You dried because you were concentrating on your own symptoms, not on serving the needs of your audience. You talked well when you forgot your own symptoms and concentrated on serving the needs of your audience."

It couldn't be that simple, he said. All great truths are simple, I said, in a burst of pomposity. And then I laid it out for him.

A A transcript of the latter half of the tape was to go to his PA immediately. The PA was to rewrite the script using his boss's *actual* words as opposed to the elegant and unsayable phrases which had been in the first version. (You see, I even caught a case of the whiches from that first version.)

B Frank was to go to his doctor in future for medical problems. Not to remove the important cues given off by his own nervous system. (See ADRENALIN, later in this chapter.)

C He was to concentrate on Saturday on making his audience feel comfortable and at ease, not on making himself feel relaxed.

D He was to deliver *content*, not unshaking hands.

"But what if I can't remember the next thing?" he said desperately, hanging on for dear life to his familiar fears.

I replayed him the bit of the tape where he had asked me to hold on while he found the figures.

"That's what you do," I told him, "you say to the audience that you're lost and would they live with you while you find yourself. If you get lost. Which you won't."

I was wrong on that one, as it turned out. On the Saturday, he got so carried away by one point he was making that when he returned to his script, he was no longer on the page he had taken off from. His PA told me that, knowing how to handle getting lost, he managed to create such a sense of delight that the audience was a bit disappointed he only got lost once.

Phyllis was younger than Frank and had a smaller audience to address; the board of the financial services institution where she was a middle manager. Her immediate boss had sent her to my company for a preparation session, I found out over an initial cup of coffee. Uh, Oh. You know the old question "Did he fall or was he pushed." When people are pushed by their bosses to seek help, then it tends to cloud their positive attitude to that help. Anyway, she said, it wasn't *she* who needed the help. I drank more coffee. When in doubt, drink coffee. The last time she had made this kind of presentation, did I know what happened? I shook an obedient head. What had happened, as it turned out, was very annoying. Phyllis had prepared her presentation, arrived on time and formally dressed, been ushered into the room (U-shaped with a central presentation area).

The senior manager in charge of the proceedings got her into position and then spoke the fatal words.

"Are you all right, Honey?" he asked.

Phyllis froze.

"I'm fine, PET," she hissed back.

The eight financial senior citizens/VIPs present, all in their fifties or older, developed a tangible rejection of her and everything she stood for, sitting silently through her presentation and devastating her with questions loaded down with references to precedents with which she could not have been expected to be familiar. Not only was the presentation a nightmare, but it was Phyllis's own conviction that her career was in stasis within the institution ever since.

I drank more coffee.

"Wasn't it an insulting way to talk to me?"

I nodded.

"Wasn't I entitled to stop him right there?"

I nodded.

"Well then," she concluded.

I went out and got fresh coffee.

"Let's talk briefly about that experience before you prepare for this immediate presentation."

"OK."

"What was your purpose in making the presentation?"

"To get them to be aware of the need for a change of corporate direction because of an emerging market."

"Did you achieve that?"

(A shrug. No.)

"Was it your purpose, before you went there, to re-educate an old man?"

"No—but—"

"Was it your purpose, before you went there, to eliminate sexism within the organisation?"

"No."

"Did you move them any closer to the elimination of sexism by what you said?"

Because she was intelligent as well as honest, she said no. Because she was courageous and positive, she then concentrated on what she wanted to achieve this time around, which was the setting up of a separate division to meet the niche market which was now self-evident, but still uncatered for.

After her presentation, her boss rang me to tell me I must have worked for several days with her, because she was so polished, so quietly confident and so (here was the killer) "lacking in stridency." I didn't tell her boss that I spent a little over an hour with her, that the material she presented was not vastly different to what she had offered them on a previous occasion, and that the repositioning she had achieved was a matter of personal decision and had nothing to do with externals. She now runs the division the set-up of which she advocated on that occasion and a man calling her or any of her female employees Honey can expect to see his career in stasis for quite some time.

In the same week that Phyllis appeared for a little over an hour, David booked in for four early morning sessions, 7 until 8.30. He told our technician that he would arrive at 6.15, because he would have a lot of technical stuff to set up. This dawn start made him as welcome to the technical staff as an outbreak of spotted mange, but at 7 on the Monday, David was ready to go. Wow, was he ready to go. He had computerised graphics on a tiny screen in front of him that fed up behind him. He had a small personal version of Autocue. He had an extraordinary little device that pretended to be a Parker pen until he wanted to emphasise a particular point, at which stage he pressed a button and it unfolded and developed a light on its further end.

"Where could I buy one of those?" I asked.

"Hey, do you like it? Do you? I'll get you one."

I didn't tell him that I thought it would be a great birthday present for my ten year old nephew.

"Do you like the slides? Do you?" he asked excitedly, "Do you see what I can do? I can just push this button here and—"

I prayed for a power cut. Three minutes into his presentation, I prayed for a blackout, personal and electrical. After five minutes, I stopped him and pulled the plug out of the wall. Everything whined away to silence and blankness, including David.

"I don't understand the point about the receivables," I said into the welcome silence.

His hands fluttered involuntarily towards the Autocue machine.

"No, just explain it to me."

He moved to sort through the electronic graphics.

"No, just explain it to me."

He stood there in a puddle of silence.

"I don't understand it myself. I can't explain it."

It was an interesting problem. David was a marketing man who had been head-hunted by a long-established service company to kick some life into their public persona and into their sales. Because he was a civilised and open man, he set out to learn all about the company first. His "mentor" was the man who expected to get David's job, and who set about explaining to him how very different this company was and how very peculiar and special its market was and how David would never really come to terms with it, but he, the mentor, would take care of it all for him. No, this idea of David's wouldn't work. Not in this company, it wouldn't. Never had. Never would. No, that idea had been tried before. Failed then, too.

David had been so overwhelmed by his introductory "briefing" from this man that in preparing his report to the major shareholders, he had focused, not on content, but on peripherals. He was putting technology and visuals out in front of him in the belief they would shield him from hostility and serve as a substitute for any real content. It looked to me that the most likely outcome of all of it was that although he might come home with his shield, he was much more likely to come home ON it, an electronic Stoic.

He took several steps backward, mentally. Revived several of the key beliefs his "mentor" had trodden on. Did a little more research, without the mentor's help. Paid for and sent back all the equipment, and eventually did his talk with four cards and a great deal of passion and conviction, heated by a modicum of retrospective resentment against his erstwhile "helper," who subsequently was found to be thinking positively about early retirement.

Three different people. Each one of whom did presentations that changed the way individuals thought and companies operated. Not because they had developed any particularly slick communication skills, but because they had stopped concentrating on peripherals and had taught themselves to keep their eye on the ball and their mind on the main objective.

The single peripheral factor most likely to take a speaker's mind off his or her main objective is nervousness.

Nervousness is like the weather. There is always a lot of it around, and it varies from a light drizzle to a hurricane. Also it is geographically widespread. Guests in TV and radio studios assume that presenters and comperes never suffer from it at all, which is usually untrue, although endless practice may dim the sharp edges a little. Nevertheless the presenter coping with a tentative interviewee on a subject the presenter knows little about, dealing with incoming telephone calls, slotting in discs and commercial breaks, and listening all the while to the instructions of the producer over his/her headphones, is often a great deal more nervous than he/she appears.

Nerves before a performance are a necessary prelude. Only bad actors do not suffer nerves before a performance. Going out in front of 700 strangers in funny clothes is an intensely artificial and challenging activity. Going out in front of 200 of your business peers in your own clothes to try to convince them of something is also a deeply challenging activity. So your hands get wet and cold. Your knees shake. Your mouth dries up. Worst of all, you notice all these things and decide you are no good and you are going to be no good today, because speakers who are any good don't suffer these kinds of symptoms, do they?

Yes. They do. Yes, they should. Yes, they continue to suffer them as long as they are called upon to speak in public. The day they stop suffering from the symptoms of nerves is the day they have got too comfortable—and that's the day the thing will go wrong.

All of the symptoms of nerves, which vary greatly between individuals, are advance warnings that the fight-or-flight hormone, adrenalin, is coming into your system. An important hormone, this. Any asthmatic who has ever got a really bad attack is likely to have been given—very, very slowly—an adrenalin injection, and to have developed, as well as clearer breathing, a sense of enormous power and potential. With enough adrenalin in your system, you get the feeling that you could write a great novel before tea-time—having first of all run a fast marathon. Adrenalin came into play back in prehistoric times when cave dwellers encountered people-eating monster animals who happened to be in a shirty mood at the time. The cave dweller got ready to fight like hell or run like hell. Anybody who has rubbed their sweaty shaking paws down the side of their skirt or trouser-covered thigh before making a major speech knows precisely how that feels.

Talking in an acoustically controlled goldfish-bowl to millions of unseen listeners or viewers is an even more intensely artificial experience, and so guests on radio and television programmes tend to be extremely nervous. Some of them manage to control their terror so that it is apparent only to themselves. Some are visibly frightened, but do not admit it. And a few have full scale attacks of terror on the spot. I have twice had people faint on me in radio studios. Curiously, both fainters, having, as they felt, gone through the very worst they had ever imagined could happen them, became quite relaxed and went on to several more appearances.

In both cases, the old rule came into play—it is the presenter's job to keep the show going, even if the roof falls in. It is a factor worth remembering. The whole show does not depend on you, so do not be more nervous than you actually need to be.

Perhaps the best single weapon in the fight against nerves is proper preparation. If you have some subject that you feel strongly about, and have prepared (see chapter six) several things to say about it, then you can focus on that subject, and your own immediate problems of dry mouth, shaky knees and wobbling wrists seem less important. The more you focus on the symptoms of your fear, the worse they get. If you begin to realise that your throat feels as if it is closing up, then thinking about it will make it close even faster.

Give yourself something to do. Re-read your preparatory notes, work out in your head which point you hope to come to first. Get yourself a drink or ask for one. In theory, every studio is supposed to have drinking water for the guests, but in practice, the carafe may be mislaid. Someone will happily supply you with water if you ask for it—or, if there is time, the very act of walking to the water fountain and filling out your own drink may help you to relax a little. Remember always that the first twenty seconds of an interview or performance are the worst. After that, it takes on a momentum of its own, and you will largely forget the terror. Getting through that first twenty seconds requires that you have something to say. It can be made very difficult by a tacky mouth and a tongue that adheres to the hard palate every time you say a word. So get yourself a drink and sip it when you feel like it. Some people find that their nervousness takes the shape of an urgent and repetitive need to clear the throat. A throat pastille may help—you can always slide the thing into a tissue once you are launched.

Terror often causes people to hyper-ventilate. They take a

series of tiny breaths, which do not satisfy the blood's need for oxygen and, as a result, they feel dizzy and sick. While you are waiting for action to happen, take big slow breaths and concentrate on getting all of the air out as well as filling your lungs in the first place.

People with allergies tend to react badly to both the excitement and the conditions of broadcasts. By conditions I mean the recycled air, the heat (television lights are extremely hot and bright) and the powder and hairspray of the makeup room. It is standard practice for many allergy sufferers to ward off an attack of, say, red patches on the skin by taking anti-histamines. For broadcast purposes, this is very dangerous. One of the most spectacular broadcasting disasters (barring the famous "the fleet's lit up" commentary) that I have ever heard was that perpetrated by an ordinarily superb BBC newsreader who did his reading one night under the influence of anti-histamines taken to combat hay fever. Pirated cassette versions are now collector's items. The reader started slurred, had a go at some complicated statistics, refused, came around the back and tried again, fell, and finally came to a giggling and unsatisfactory compromise. Within seconds, another voice had cut in, and the newsreader was off the air—for three months. Anti-histamines (and any cough medicine or other medication carrying the usual warning to the effect that "this may cause drowsiness. If affected, do not drive or operate machinery") should not be taken before a broadcast. The strangeness of the situation may cause them to react badly, even if they normally have little or no effect, and there is also the factor that many people cannot eat before an important broadcast, and so the medicine can run riot on an empty stomach.

Alcohol and tranquillisers are both very tempting, but should not be taken. In the early days of television, the "hospitality suite" was always open before major live programmes because it was believed that a few drinks before a programme relaxed everybody and loosened the tongue so that effortless conversation flowed. A few spectacular contradictions of that caused broadcasting organisations to cut back severely on the time given to drinking before programmes, and indeed many shows go on the air now with their participants awash in nothing more lethal than tea and sympathy. And a very good thing too. There are arguably more alcoholics in show-business than in any other walk of life, and it is extremely hard on someone with a drink problem to watch other people, who do not have a problem, sloshing back alcohol before an experience which is full of stress. More to the point, the person who takes a couple of scoops before a programme, then goes on and is superb, does not become less nervous when the next programme comes along. He just becomes more certain that alcohol was the secret of success, and so a very bad dependency is set up.

Many experienced broadcasters advise newcomers to take one drink, and only one drink. My own belief is that if one drink relaxes you, the logic is that two drinks will relax you even more, and three drinksh will have yousho relazxshed thzatzyou dongivadam. Save the alcohol for afterwards, and you will have all of your terrified wits about you, which, after all, is the primeval function of nervousness.

And then there are tranquillisers. A true story about tranquillisers. Some time ago, I was working with a production team of eleven people, filming a short play for use in mental health discussions. The theme of the drama was the drug-addicted married woman, and the actress involved was called upon to spill a bottle of Valium at the breakfast table.

The actress came to the sequence, overturned the bottle and someone said "Valium don't look like that." Saccharin tablets were filling in for the drug.

"That's right," someone else said. "They're smaller."

"And thinner," said a third voice.

"Like this," said a fourth, holding out a vial.

"Mine look fatter, " a fifth said, pulling a bottle out of a breastpocket.

It turned out that five of the eleven people involved were taking the tranquilliser. Now certainly these were creative people working to deadlines under a lot of pressure in a temperamental business. But the problem is that when so many people are taking Valium and Librium, or their equivalent, to make it through the normal strains of the day, it makes it difficult to advise against their use for the quite extraordinary strains of first TV and radio appearances.

The difficulty about tranquillisers is that they damp down excitement, and you respond more slowly to all sorts of stimuli, including, in the interview or panel programme situation, the stimulus of fear and exhilaration. There is the added danger that your speech may be slightly slower, or have the distinctive dry-mouth sound of the habitual trank-taker. If you are on medically prescribed tranquillisers as a matter of course, then your doctor's advice should be followed. If you normally do not take tranquillisers, then, when some well meaning soul offers you "just a Roche Five," thank him or her, but do not take up the offer.

If you are regularly involved in public appearances in the way of your work, or for some other reason, and you find that nervousness is likely to cause you problems, then it is well worth investigating, and if necessary investing in, some long-term therapy for your fear.

Yoga, hypnotism, or a complete set of muscle relaxant exercises can help if nerves become a major obstacle to ease in public appearances. One of the things which can be very useful is if, in the thirty seconds before you are due to start, you concentrate on cramping every muscle in your body over which you have conscious control so hard that it hurts. Your hands are clenched, your toes screwed up in your shoes, your calves bunched and your stomach knotted. Hold it like that until it becomes acutely painful. Then relax all those agonised muscles and go to the podium. Many speakers find that their muscles are so relieved to get out of clench that they don't remember how nervous they are—and go back INTO clench—until the talk is well begun. And once a talk is underway, nerves lessen, anyway. There is an unspoken rule which holds that about 45 seconds into an interview or presentation, a wonderful feeling of survival comes over the speaker, and nerves recede considerably.

I hesitate to pass on any physical methods of coping with the symptoms of nerves, because it tends to suggest a) that nerves are a bad thing and b) that you should spend time preventing them.

On the contrary, you should be concentrating on the first key point you wish to make to the people present. After you have greeted them.

It's an odd thing, but if I were asked to name the single most frequent discourtesy committed by public speakers, it is that they do not greet their auditors civilly. They may go through the dignitaries listed on the page in front of them. "Madam Chairman, My Lord Bishop, Mr Chancellor, the group from the Geesespotting Association, Ladies and Gentlemen." But they read it off the page, with their eyes glued to the page. Let it be stated here as an absolute. Even if you cannot take your eyes off the page for the rest of the presentation, you *must* look warmly and welcomingly at the people in front of you when you say "Ladies and Gentlemen." Better still if you can make your first point while you're looking at them. Come ON. Your first point? See, it worked. Now that you've made your first point and glanced down to see where you go from there, try making your second point to them as well. People tend to hear you better when they can see you better, and they can see you better when they can see your eyes. (If you don't believe me about hearing better when you can see better, ask any shortsighted friend of yours. They'll tell you that they can't hear you properly until the get their specs on.) If you have gone to the trouble of preparing a speech then it is surely worth the extra effort to make them feel at home and to make them feel that you don't regard them as a row of cabbages.

You will, of course, encounter communications trainers who will tell you that row of cabbages is precisely how you should see your audience. It amazes me that this one survives. Nobody I know has ever wanted to talk to a cabbage on an intimate one-to-one basis. Your average cabbage lacks a lot as a conversationalist. Sure, it's a good listener, but you can never change its mind or get a laugh. Or even annoy it.

When you're talking in public, those watching you are not to be insulted by treatment as cabbages. (Or mushrooms, and you know what they say about *them*.) They are individuals, with individual minds, individual imaginations and individual life patterns. They do not become a mass just because they happen to sit down in a single location with a great many other individuals.

You must talk to them as individuals. At any one moment, you are only talking to one person—all the others are listening in. Talk to the individuals you can see—but don't stay talking to any one of them. You will find that some nod. Or smile. Or otherwise react. You may find useful signals coming up from them. Signals that say "you've lost me, that got complicated" or "you've made that point, don't beat me to death with it, get on to the next thing." Communication should always be a genuinely two-way thing, and it can only be that if you watch and talk to the individuals who make up your audience. Never mind the appalling jargon which has been developed around this basic human courtesy ("four-eye contact" is just one of the more repellent phrases that Americans use for it). Just keep your eyes on the people you're talking to except when you really do need to look at your notes.

Don't be guilty or hurried about looking at your notes. Your attitude must be that you have prepared valuable information for the use of this particular group and you need the time to refer to it in order to quote it accurately. Remember, that time passing as perceived by the audience is much shorter than time passing as perceived by the speaker. What feels like ten minutes of agonising fumble to you looks, to the audience, like a momentary hesitation.

If you are lost, at any stage in front of an audience, that is not a problem. When it becomes a problem is when you try to pretend you are not lost. You don't know what the last thing you said was, you don't know what is the next thing you're going to say, you don't know what page you're on or what page the next helpful clue will be, but gosh, no, you're not lost. LOST? Shucks! How could you be lost?

When this happens, you are so busy pretending not to be lost that you cannot give the time needed to find yourself. Your anxiety is instantly conveyed to the audience, who immediately become restive. The simple and infallible way around this problem is to admit to being lost. Admit it to yourself and to the audience. You are then not anxious, because you have bought time to find yourself in, and they are not anxious because you have told them you'll have your act together in a couple of seconds. Afterwards, they will remember how cool you were, not how lost you were.

I have to confess that I discovered this by accident years ago, when I worked, briefly in the theatre. I was on stage one night in a revue, getting launched on the second verse of a parody when I suddenly realised that I couldn't remember the words. The pianist, in mid-oompah, looked up, startled, when noise did not come out of me, and went around the musical block to do another oompah. The other actors, all concentrating on their own parts, didn't even notice.

I flagged down the pianist.

"People," I said democratically to the audience. "I've lost the words. Hold on a sec." Assuming this was another joke, they held on a sec.

"What are the right words?" I asked the actor nearest to me onstage.

"Jesus, I don't know," he said honestly. "It's YOUR song."

This got an unexpected laugh and, at the same moment, the right words occurred to me and we resumed. At the end of the song, I got an individual round of applause which I had never won before for this particular ditty—and a subsequent warning from other members of the cast not to try THAT attention-grabber again. I could not convince them that I had genuinely dried.

"Yeah," one of them growled. "And got a standing ovation just by accident!"

The moral of my story is that if you try to be phony with an audience, they know you for what you are, whereas if you tell them you're sorting yourself out, you have not projected your problem on to them, but you have included them in your performance.

Keeping your eye on the audience is a good thing. But where do you keep your hands? Hands are the oddest things. They can be useful or useless. W.B. Yeats was so convinced that hands were useless to Irish actors that he once remarked that he wished he could have the hands of the actors in Ireland's National

Theatre encased with the rest of them in barrels, so that only their faces could be visible.

There is no single cast-iron rule about hands. Well, perhaps one. If your hands are useful to you, if you are the sort of person who talks with their hands, then you should make sure that they can be useful to you in public speaking. By that I mean that you should not sit or stand in such a position that your hands are locked in place and unavailable to you. Some people I know feel helpless if they have to hold a script; they need a podium to put the script on and then they can let their hands gesture freely. On the other hand, I know speakers who use their script as an extra prop, flailing it, rolling it up and thumping it into the other open hand. On one marvellous occasion, I watched a man make a very funny self-derogatory speech about his various failings as an industrialist, public figure, husband and father.

He concluded by indicating that, having delivered this speech, he had now lost confidence in it, too, and made to tear it up. However, because it was made up of a fair number of pages and because he had folded it over prior to tearing, it would not tear. He struggled frantically with it for a couple of moments, and bent it quite some, but no satisfying rags resulted.

"See?" he said plaintively to the audience, and brought the house down.

Be very wary of learning specific gesture types. There is a pseudo science abroad which suggests that everybody should learn horizontal and lateral gestures and develop the capacity to deliver them at different paces, and that this adds up to a stunning, but essentially subliminal extra element in the public speaker's armoury. Hogwash. The only technical advice anybody should pay attention to in general terms about gestures is that they should come from the shoulder, not from the elbow. Gestures that start from the elbow tend to be physically tight and diminish the point made. Only when you develop an annoying pattern of gestures do you need to interfere with the way your hands move. Remember when you first learned to drive a car, you thought that you would never get the gear stick right and you had to make a separate choice each and every time you changed gear as to whether you would, afterward, leave your hand on the gear stick, put it in your lap or hang onto the steering wheel with it. Now, if you have been driving for a number of years, your hands do what they're supposed to do; help you with driving. They do not get ideas about their own importance, and you do not wonder if you should get them separate tuition as driving hands.

Most people would much rather discuss learning tricks for their hands than discipline for their eyes. It is much easier to learn a marvellous chopping gesture for your right hand than it is to develop the practice of watching the audience while you're talking to them. Many potentially great speakers are convinced that the audience is The Enemy and that it knows something about the speaker which is very bad. Either it knows it, or it's going to catch the speaker doing something very bad.

An audience is never trying to catch you doing something wrong. An audience is much more eager to catch you doing something right. Even if they have nothing in common with you and no previous commitment to your views.

Not so long ago I was in an audience of urban dwellers being addressed by a number of people about credit problems. One of them was a farmer, and as he got up to talk I'm sure it crossed his mind to assume that we city-folk were rejecting him in advance and filled with the expectation that he would come with a tissue of complaints, because that's what farmers do, don't they?

Not in this instance, they didn't. The man was a potato farmer, and he talked about some boom years he had experienced and how they had enabled him to borrow heavily in order to build a state-of-the-art potato storage silo. It was completed, commissioned and duly filled. The speaker told the story of how he had gone out to the store on the 20th of December for a quiet gloat.

I opened the doors and the first thing that struck me was that the potatoes had gone down. Not much. A few inches. But they had sunk. And that meant only one thing. Decomposition. They were sinking down into each other. Blight. And there was nothing I could do about it. They were finished. My whole year's work. My time. My family's time. My investment. My future. All gone, because of a few inches dropped. I stood there and I did up a little plan in my mind. Long-term, I knew it was going to be a disaster. But short-term, we could get through Christmas if I didn't tell anybody. So I closed the doors and I didn't tell my wife until the 28th of December and at least Christmas was OK.

Because he had not wasted time on peripherals (I don't know what gestures his hands produced), because he had not wasted time on bad thoughts about the audience (he just looked at us as he told the story) and because he told something he felt strongly about in details only he could have known (the few inches of lost volume), he won us, informed us and changed the way we thought, not just about credit, but about farmers generally.

Chapter Six

Making a Media Appearance

Any person who can't explain his work to a fourteen
year-old is a charlatan.

Nobel Prize winning chemist, *Dr Irving Langmuir*

If your house blows up, if you invent something by accident, or
if a masked man leaps out of the woodwork to steal from you,
the News on radio or television may want to interview you.

If your business is going through particularly interesting
times, or if you are either leading a public protest or the target
of a public protest, then you may be asked to appear on a
Current Affairs or Features programme. If you have made a
major announcement or have recently published a book, you
may be offered the opportunity to appear on a chat show.

No matter what the programme, the first thing you need to
do is ask questions. This is not what most people do. Most
people say "yes" and then panic.

"What am I going to say?" they then think. "What'll they ask
me? Will they give me any chance to talk? Will it be a
disaster?"

You wonder why they agreed to appear. Perhaps you wonder
aloud why they agreed to appear. They'll tell you they had no
choice. Why not? They'll shrug and indicate that if they refused
to appear, the presenter might say, to the camera, that the
programme had asked a representative of the Bloggs company
to appear, but the Bloggs company hadn't been able to see their

way to send someone along. The person from Bloggs & Co invariably says this as if it were an open and shut diagnosis. You have to appear, because if you don't they will say you refused. What Bloggs & Co never seem to address is the possibility that by appearing they may do much more damage than by not appearing. Let's face it, it takes no more than a couple of seconds for a presenter to announce the non-appearance of the Bloggs representative. If the Bloggs man goes on a major TV current affairs programme and makes a dog's breakfast of his input, the disaster in visible, memorable and lengthy. Given that possibility, Bloggs should seriously consider how *contained* and limited damage done by a non-appearance may be better than wide-screen, technicolour, personalised and brand name damage done by an appearance.

It's a choice between two evils. It's a choice which is different every time because of the company involved and the story being explored. But it is a choice, and the best choices are always made on the basis of good information. So before you say "yes" or "no" you need to ask questions drawn from the list that follows. And if you don't like the answers, don't miss an opportunity to shut up.

How Long Will the Item Last?

If you know that a TV discussion is to fill twenty minutes, then you have a clear idea of the pressures that will be on you. If, on the other hand, you're going on a TV news programme, it focuses your mind to know that the interview has been allotted only two minutes of broadcast time.

Going into a TV or radio studio in the belief that the entire programme is to be devoted to a particular item, or that it will be the 'main' item, without knowing roughly how long the discussion is planned to last, may leave you contributing too much or too little, and resentful about it at the end. Be clear, however, that the timings they may give you will be approximate. They may not decide until just before the programme the exact length of time, or they may leave it open-ended, so that if it develops into something worth extending they will add to the time devoted to it.

If you are going on a news programme, the item will be shorter than if you are going on a features or current affairs programme. Interviews which feature in TV and radio news bulletins, for example, are often shorter than half a minute, even though as much as ten minutes of material may have been recorded. The programme editor picks the bit that most suits the item—from his point of view—and chops off the rest. The trend is towards short, rather than long. In the USA the average broadcast time of an interview in a news bulletin is 11 seconds. Interviewees go on, knowing that they are officially known as a "sound bite." Not a meal. Not a mouthful—a bite. You get 11 seconds and you have to be good for 11 seconds.

(Increasingly, too, on the other side of the Atlantic, the tendency is for the interviewer to talk with the interviewee without the cameras rolling for long enough to establish the single answer targeted by the crew. This obviates the need to record and subsequently edit a lengthy interview, and, although it adds pressure on the interviewee to be vivid and succinct, it also eliminates the resentment often experienced by interviewees who talk for 10 minutes only to see 10 seconds of them at their weakest selected for programme use.)

Why Am I Being Asked?

The answer may be obvious. But it is not always so. Let's say for example that you are a member of a trade association affected by a Government ruling, newly announced. The morning TV current affairs programme asks you to appear. You are flattered. But why is the head of your association not being asked? Have they sought you out as a maverick to come out with stronger comments than your association may think proper?

Without false modesty, it may occur to you as you talk over the possibility of appearing, that there is someone better qualified than you to talk on the subject. Say so. It may well be that the other person is over-exposed, or that the producer simply thinks you are a better talker. Just get things clear in advance. It is also useful if they know your views, so that they will not be disappointed when you turn out to be sweetly reasonable when they expected a colourful diehard.

Sometime, people are asked to appear on radio and TV programmes because a researcher or producer remembers them from a previous appearance. If the last time you were on, you believed the something you believe in now, all is well. If, however, you have changed attitude, political party or company, it may be worth mentioning this to the person inviting you to be there.

Who's Interviewing?

This is not a desperately important question, but it is probably the first thing most interviewees would like to ask. Once you have got the answer do not start trying to figure out his/her prejudices, political views, hang-ups or sore points. They are none of your business. Knowing them will make you uneasy and unnatural, because you will be concentrating on the presenter's job instead of your own. The very fact of seeking the information will make you paranoid.

The interviewer may be a person who takes a lively antagonistic posture in studio. An "I put it to you" man. Like America's Sean Donaldson.

Donaldson states in his autobiography *Hold on, Mr President*

> If you send me to cover a pie-baking contest on Mother's Day, I'm going to ask dear old Mom whether she used artificial sweeteners in violation of the rules, and, while she's at it, could I see the receipt for the apples to prove she didn't steal them. I maintain that if Mom has nothing to hide, no harm will have been done.

In other words "nothing personal Mom."

Let's put the position from the interviewee's side. The interviewee agrees to go on the programme because he has something worth saying. Something the viewing or listening audience should hear. In that context, the interviewer is like a telephone: merely the instrument facilitating the communication between Party A and Party B. Nobody in advance of a phone call, worries about the pedigree and personal passions of the phone. Even an unusual appearance (Mickey Mouse or Edwardian Crystal) are momentary distractions. Basically, the caller talks to the person being called, and the phone is just *there*. Similarly, the interviewer is just there and you should not waste your time trying to figure out his hidden agenda, or fight with him on the air.

What's the Item Preceded By?

Occasionally, items in current affairs programmes are preceded by film clips. Among the possible introductory clips is a segment of street interviews with unnamed passers-by. These are known as "vox pops" and are a useful and colourful way of introducing a subject. They are, however, rarely objective. Sometimes "vox pops" may indicate that the public know nothing about the subject in hand and care less, or that they are, in the main, hostile to one side of the argument or another. The production team will not deliberately pick a biased selection. However, they will certainly seek an emotive and lively selection, the objective being to pick people with a view to creating shock, amusement or fury in the audience. If you are the interviewee following this clip, it helps to have seen them beforehand or at least have had the contents outlined to you, so that you can begin to think along the lines presented. Usually, the production team will be happy to have you informed so that you can do a better job for them. In the rare instance where they are not co-operative, you must ask yourself *why* they are not, and, as a corollary, whether or not you should go on their programme. They can get other guests, and they will have another programme next week. You, on the other hand, have to live for a long time with whatever impression of yourself and your views is left with the watching public.

Who Else Is Appearing?

If someone with an opposing viewpoint to yours is going to be on the programme, well and good. It means that you must prepare for a non-compliant audience for your comments, and this may help you to firm up your thinking and concentrate your preparation time before the broadcast. On the other hand, there is an outside chance that someone will be appearing who might give you problems, either because they are so utterly unpredictable or because there is personal animus between you. If someone is included whose presence would interfere with your doing a good job, indicate politely that you cannot go along, and if possible suggest someone else to take your place.

Will There Be Phone Calls?

The "phone-in" is one of the cheapest and liveliest radio formats. Assured of anonymity, people ring radio programmes to protest, comment and query. They do it without having to be paid fees, and they will often fight with programme participants. TV and radio producers are increasingly playing the numbers game in the sense of selling audiences achieved to advertisers. ("Looka, our show gets 23.2% of all literate teenagers who aren't high at the time, and they spend £2.67 per day on hamburgers. You want to advertise your hamburgers on our show?!) Because of the numbers game, attracting audiences as cheaply as possible is a priority, and having a fight on the air is one sure way of doing it. In the U.S., a man names Downey has developed what can only be called Diatribe Television where famous people submit themselves to public and extraordinarily distasteful drubbing, because they seem unable to turn down the chance of appearing on the box. Diatribe Television is increasingly infiltrating radio, where in the guise of an inappropriate marriage of free speech and controversy, racists, anti-feminists, terrorists and other enraged and intemperate people are given air time. The end result is frequently very frank, worrying—in that some of the material covered tends to exacerbate rather than "explore" tensions— and is extremely popular. Although there is less of this kind of thing on this side of the Atlantic, there is a growing tendency for programme-makers to set up a VIP in the role of Aunt Sally. Come throw your coconuts, folks, today our guest is…

Some people not only survive the Aunt Sally treatment but relish it. Those people tend to be well-briefed, confident and to have jobs where a decision made on the air will not subsequently be backed out of by a board of directors or other group.

What's the Item Sandwiched Between?

This question is not relevant if you are being asked on a news or current affairs programme. However, many people are touchy about going on chat shows because they say that a serious subject cannot be discussed in such a context. This is simply not true. It is certainly a challenge, given TV's tendency to provoke dog-fights as opposed to reasoned debates, but good speakers with strong feelings and the courage to voice their opinions clearly and simply (see Chapter Seven) can do a very good job of handling a serious subject on this type of programme. But it is an individual decision all of the time. If you are asked to discuss abortion for ten minutes in between fifteen minutes devoted to a man who keeps ferrets in his trousers, and, at the other end of the abortion item, a woman who can toss tassels on her breasts anti-clockwise, then you must be clear on the limitations under which you will be operating, if you agree to go on.

When you have asked all of these questions, the next thing to do is find out how soon the production people need a Yes or a No. This depends on the kind of programme. A chat show which is considering your inclusion four weeks from now may want you to accept or refuse their invitation within ten days. A news programme going out this evening may want your acceptance or refusal within ten minutes, or, better still, from their point of view, immediately if not sooner. Ask them. Even if they want an immediate response, tell them you need a couple of minutes to think it over, and that you'll ring them back within a quarter of an hour, or that they can ring you within that time.

So you have ten minutes thinking time. You put down the phone and you do some fast, heavy-duty thinking.

You do that thinking with one thing in mind. You don't HAVE to go on. You can refuse. Most people, invited to appear on television programmes, are so overwhelmed by media-itis that they forget that it isn't like the old days of pre-revolutionary France, when a *lettre de cachet* was an invitation to the Bastille which could not be refused. So they go on programmes where they are insulted, denigrated and given no time to think or talk. The most extreme version of this type of programming is one presented in the US by one Morton Downey. On this side of the Atlantic, public surgery without anaesthetic is done with more finesse. Dr. Anthony Clare's *In the Psychiatrist's Chair* interviewing style has all the civilised erudition Downey's lacks. The general feeling left by one of his programmes is that he has given his interviewee a very persistent series of pokes in the chest and other tender parts with a very clean index finger, whereas Downey bludgeons them about the head with a heavy dirty sledgehammer. Nevertheless, Clare shrinks from asking no question, nor does he back off when the person he is questioning comes up with a fast facile explanation.

"But why do you SAY that?" Clare will pursue. "What does that MEAN?"

For some people, *In the Psychiatrist's Chair* has been an exciting opportunity for public self-analysis and affirmation in company with a lively, sceptical enquirer. For others, it has been a disaster.

Are There People I Should Consult?

Think quickly. (You have perhaps five minutes left.) If you work for a company, then your boss may have to know. Or your board. Or the public relations officer, who may become a little fraught if you go on television unexpectedly and say something about which he has no warning and which may require subsequent mopping of blood or adding of fuel to newly-lit flames. Hell hath no fury to match a PRO dropped in it while the media watch, and public confusion does not lead to your company becoming corporate flavour of the month. If you are a politician (see pages 163-171) you have to obey very specific rules, unless you are a happy freewheeling Independent, in which case you are agin everything and don't need to notify anybody except perhaps your mother.

Sometimes, you need to take legal advice before you go on television. If a case is controversial but *sub judice,* you will need legal advice before you agree to go on. Generally, lawyers advise against appearing where there are any fine legal lines to be trodden.

Friends, family, members of an association or neighbours may all be relevant for advance warning. In some cases, you will want to ask them if they think you should appear, or what they think you should say if you DO appear. In other cases, you will just want to give them fair warning. If, at breakfast time, someone rings you to compliment you on that fact that your twenty year old son came out of the closet and confessed to being a life-long cross-dresser on last night's *Upfront Chat Show,* you can feel an outsize fool if your son never told you he was going to do it.

Can I See the Questions in Advance?

The short answer here should be no. You are certainly entitled to know the general areas which will be covered, but only an inept interviewer will be in a position to provide you with the wording of the questions to be asked, because any interviewer worth a damn does not operate from a pre-packaged list. Good interviewers know what they want to get, in the way of information, reactions or confirmations. The wording of the questions designed to get what they are after should emerge as part of the process. The most dangerous questions are the simplest ones. The most probing questions are the ones following an interviewee's statements; questions like "Why do you say that?" "Explain how that fits with your previous record?" Any fool can think up a good question. It takes a great interviewer to think up a good supplementary and ask it at the right time. So don't waste your energies asking for a list of questions. You shouldn't want one. They shouldn't give you one. And if they do, the interviewer shouldn't stick to it, because if that's the way interviews happen on television, it's a ready-up which puts the ordinary licence paying viewer at a disadvantage.

I don't mind you having Joe Soap on the programme, but I don't want to be on at the same time.
Now we're into power games. If you are a lay-person with a bit of expertise, it is unlikely that the TV crew will listen to this kind of request from you, never mind accede to it. However, politicians when they get into Government are notorious for doing it. There are Ministers who never sit with the Opposition spokesperson, live, in the same TV studio, because they believe it would put them under too much pressure, or they feel it might promote the Opposition figure to a prominence the Minister seeks to deny. The Ministers who do this end up with too many boring programme slots because there is no conflict, and television loves conflict. The only time I advise clients to seek to be interviewed on their own is where the other potential panellist is unpredictably unprofessional. They are few and far between, these unpredictable non-professionals, but they exist, and if you know that someone is due to appear on a programme with you who is likely to be drunk or whose name has been made by being obnoxious to people, serious thought should be given to seeking a separate slot within the programme. If the producer cannot agree, then you have to think seriously if the risks outweigh the advantages.

Can I Talk to the Interviewer in Advance?
It isn't always possible, and it is rarely as important as you think it may be. You need to know the programme brief. You don't need to be bosom buddies with the interviewer. If you are very shortsighted, or hard of hearing, you should also let them know. The man who is rather deaf in his right ear has only

himself to blame if the interview is conducted by someone sitting on his right, and therefore inaudible to him. A quick word will ensure a switch of seats.

Will The Interviewer Give Me Time If I Stammer?

Stammering is both a problem and an advantage to an interviewee. It depends on the stammer. The stammer which is utterly out of control is disabling and worrying in a radio or TV studio. The stammer with which its owner has come to an accommodating relationship can be quite acceptable and may help in attracting attention. Patrick Campbell, the man whose stutter became so popular that he was eventually paid to stutter in advertising commercials, tells in his autobiography of his very first broadcast.

> Before we went on, David Frost asked me if I'd like him to say something about my stammer when he was introducing me. I agreed with him that it might be a good idea to prepare the audience for the shock of being faced with a talker who couldn't speak, for by now I was certain I'd be unable to articulate a single word.
>
> I'd have given anything to be able to get up and walk out of the studio. I felt sick at the thought of my own vanity, the vanity that had led me to believe that I could perform with professionals in public.
>
> The show began. David introduced me by saying something like "And now, here is Patrick Campbell, who may or may not be able to speak," and suddenly I got the most extraordinary feeling of euphoria. I was still tense and excited, but I couldn't wait to try and get the first laugh from the studio audience. I felt they were warm and friendly and on my side.

An audience is always warm to someone who has a physical problem and is neither pretending it's not there nor seeking sympathy because it IS there. A producer will be helpful if you give notice of any factor which needs management in the interests of your giving a good performance and providing him with good programme value.

There are other, more personal modifiers you may need to seek. An interviewee once asked, in my presence, for a guarantee that he would not be asked about his drinking. Since the programme a) had nothing to do with alcohol, and b) was likely to have him on the ropes on a quite different subject, this was an unthreatening surprise. The producer shrugged.

"Why?"

"Because it has nothing to do with the programme you're making, and because I'm a member of AA. I know there are lots of well-known people these days who trumpet about the fact that they're alcoholics, but I take the AA's anonymity thing very seriously."

Although the interviewer went after him ruthlessly on the programme, she never mentioned alcohol. It was an individual modification sought in a particular situation, and a producer made a decision which died with the programme.

A quite different modifier happened when a current affairs programme was setting out to expose as crooked the workings of a particular entrepreneur. He decided that he had no choice but to go on the programme to defend himself, and duly arrived at the TV station. Made up and ushered into the studio, he suddenly baulked.

"Hold it," he said stopping dead the moment he walked around the studio cyclorama.

"Is there something wrong?" the floor manager asked.

"Mmm," the entrepreneur said, retreating behind the big curtain again. This move baffled the floor manager, who could not be expected to know that the entrepreneur's paranoia level was so high that he was not going to utter a recordable word or allow the development of a facial expression within spitting distance or either a camera or a microphone. The entrepreneur retreated along the space between the studio curtain and the wall until he backed out the door into the corridor, pursued by a floor manager who was simultaneously trying to pacify, by using his radio telephone gadget, a director enraged by the sudden dearth of humans in his studio. The entrepreneur hauled the floor manager out the studio door after him, jammed it closed, and hissed through rage-gritted teeth.

"I'm not stupid," he told the floor manager. "I know bloody well what you're trying to do to me with that set and I won't let you away with it."

"What are we trying to do?" the floor manager asked, praying that someone in more authority than he was would come and rescue him from the mauve-hued lump of whispering outrage.

"You're trying to say I'm rolling in money, that's what you're trying to do. Bloodywell mahogany wall panelling and a bloody great leather chair and a bloody VDU and a carpet you could sink up to your navel in. Bloated capitalist living off the fat of the land ministered to by slaves, that's what you want me to look like."

The floor manager drew a breath. It stayed drawn.

"Oil paintings, for Chrissake," the entrepreneur added in spurting rage.

At this moment, the director joined them in the corridor and the entrepreneur turned his considerable energies on him, much to the relief of the floor manager, who was white as the driven snow metaphorically and literally.

"I operate out of the back of a small four year old car," the entrepreneur told the director. "That's my office. No mahogany. No VDUs. No gold Parkers sticking out of lumps of jade. Now, if you want to be REALLY truthful, why don't ye get your cameras and come out and do the interview there?"

The director made noises about deadlines and practicalities and the difficulties of generating usable footage in the back of a small four year old car.

"I thought you mightn't want to do that," the entrepreneur said sourly. "But I'll tell you something for nothing, there is no bloody way you are getting me into a setting that tells lies about me and the way I do business, so get rid of all that crap or I'm gone."

The director denied any evil intent and pointed out that a clinically blank studio was less interesting to watch. The entrepreneur reiterated his conditions for staying and being interviewed. The director gave in. The studio was cleared and the interview eventually looked as it if had been done in an obscure corner of an empty fridge. There was certainly no impression of boundless riches.

One other example of a very personal modification sought by a programme participant came about when a programme known for its pleasant pace and easy style came to film on location in a seaside resort. A local historian was invited to participate and he greeted the invitation in a warmly positive but guarded way. Yes, he said, he would be delighted to take part as long as the interviewing was done indoors. This did not suit the director, who was keen to get crashing waves and soaring seagulls in the background. The Production Assistant shuttled to and fro between historian and director, peddling diluted versions of what each said to the other.

"Find out what's eating him and tell him it suits us better to do it on the beach," was translated as "The Director is very eager to facilitate you, but he wonders if the beach might not be a perfect location, given its association with the Norman landing?"

The curt reply "I wouldn't consider for one moment being interviewed on the beach," was translated into "He has a fairly major concern about the beach as a location and he would really prefer not to be out of doors."

Eventually, the PA, a woman of persistence and discretion, fed the historian several private cups of coffee and eventually got the truth out of him. He had recently invested in a toupee for which he had much affection, but in which he had little faith. Because he was not used to it, he was scared that it might be provoked by a breezy day into taking off for the Isle of Man without him in it, and even more scared that this departure might be recorded for all time on film. The PA promised him an indoor location, without even asking her director, and further promised him that she would manage it without revealing the reason to the entire crew. The historian gave a great interview in a suburban home where three ducks flew up a wall but no toupees flew.

So. You have agreed to go on a TV programme. You are going to appear for a live interview which is expected to last six minutes on a current affairs programme. You will be interviewed on your own. Let's look, first of all, at the kind of preparation you will need to do for that specific programme type, and then we can examine the different preparation required by variations on that type.

The Preparation Grid appeared earlier, but let's look at it now in the context of your TV interview.

What points am I going to make?	How am I going to make them?	What are the obvious questions?	What are the nasty questions?

You have six minutes at your disposal, so you should plan on making at least two and perhaps three points. If you get the chance to make a fourth, well and good, but it may be a better idea to repeat one of the earlier points using different illustrations, and there is certainly no point in giving yourself a shopping list of points you have no real possibility of making in a vivid, understandable and memorable way.

In the first column of the grid, then, you should note the two or three main points you plan to make. Let's say that you run a company that sells cars, and that the reason you have been asked to talk on the programme is because a consumer magazine has accused you of raising prices while ignoring safety.

In the left hand column, you may decide that your first point should be:

Prices not excessive—*Match inflation rate*

You then add that your second point should be *We're totally concerned with safety*.

Your third point, you then decide, should be *cheap can mean less safe*.

Now move into the second column. Put down your pen for a moment and think about that first point you want to make. You want to leave the audience with the idea that your cars are good value. So why reverse into it by a denial? The moment you deny something, you are, in effect, repeating the accusation which has been made against you. The programme may repeat the accusation but there is no good reason you should help them along. So in preparing to make that first point, get out of the gear I call Communicator's Reverse. Get to the positive point. You have a car. Its price has stayed level with inflation. OK. Tell us the name of the car. Tell us what price it was two years ago. Tell us what price it is now, and indicate how that matches the inflation rate. Try it out a few times until the details come to you in manageable chunks that anybody listening can understand first time around. Now note down the relevant details in the second column of the grid.

Having put flesh and features on the first of your points, you now move to your second one. **Totally concerned with safety.** Oh yeah? Oh yeah, you say, testily. So prove it. No assertions allowed. Put legs under the claim. Oh, you say, look at the alloy. Alloy? Your company wouldn't use the newly developed alloy because you suspect that metal fatigue will set in earlier. And also there are air bags. Air bags? Yes. Your company has them under active study and if, as seems likely, they prove to be better than seat belts because there are always people who won't wear seat belts, you'll install them along with the belts as normal. And, of course there is… Wait. Don't over-illustrate a point. Take it away from being an unsubstantiated assertion, but don't turn it into a Christmas tree. Pick the newest, most surprising, most colourful illustration; the one that will make viewers turn to each other and say "Hey, I never knew that before."

Third point is a lash at your competitors. An unsubstantiated lash is just as bad as an unsubstantiated assertion. Can you give an example of a particular car which disintegrates if it runs into a rubber plant, but is selling like hell because it is cheap?

When you have your three points fleshed out a bit, it's time to put yourself in the interviewer's place and ask the obvious questions. In order to do this, you need to do the research that the interviewer will do or will have done by a researcher.

If the interview is to be about your product, your service, or your area of expertise, you should be able to parallel the interviewer's preparation with absolute precision, so that you are in a position to predict the thrust, if not the wording, of the majority of questions asked. Take the example of yourself as CEO of this company under attack for selling costly cars. Where will you start your research? With the consumer magazine which originated the story. (That's where the TV interviewer will move next.) After that? You will figure out what vested interests related to your business are likely to say (if the interviewer has the time, he'll have them saying those things on tape.) On the basis of this rudimentary research, you first of all build up a picture, and then figure out the questions you would ask if you were an interviewer.

You'd start by reading aloud the most damning accusation in the consumer magazine and seeking a response to it.

Now, imagine that this is what has happened. How will you respond?

Let me tell you how you should NOT respond. Like this:

"Well, Mike, that's a very good question. Before I come to it, however, I want to point out to the viewers that my company, Noddy Cars Ltd., has this year introduced a new model which will…"

That answer loses you so many brownie points you could be in deficit for a year.

Lost Brownie Point 1: "Well Mike..."

Overfamiliar. And a deadly giveaway if you start by first-naming an interviewer and end up surnaming him after he has asked you the third stinker question. Don't call him anything. He knows who he is. The viewers know who he is. You don't have to stroke him by confirming his identity or making with the old pal act.

Lost Brownie Point 2: "That's a very good question..."

It isn't your job (or your right) to define what's a good question. That's for TV critics. On you, it looks like crawling.

Lost Brownie Point 3: "Before I come to that, however..."

Whatever tricky consultant told you to do this should be fired. If you picked it up from watching some smartass on TV, you admire the wrong people. The interviewer is the representative of the audience at home. The audience at home therefore have a sense of ownership of his questions. Your implying that your objectives come before those the interviewer shares with the audience at home is neither civil nor acceptable. The interviewer, if he has even baseline assertiveness, will not let you get away with it. Answer his damn question and THEN link to the first point you wanted to make.

Lost Brownie Point 4: "My company, Noddy Cars Ltd..."
There are some boards of directors and some bosses who think that mentioning a company or product name is in itself a wondrous broadcasting *tour de force* with a prodigious marketing benefit to the operation. Thalidomide and Chemie Grunenthal once got a lot of mentions without that result. Ditto, Edsel and Ford. Ditto Morton Thiokol and Challenger. Give listeners added value and don't waste their time waving bits of corporate bunting.

Losing five points on your first answer is surprisingly easy. You can lose a sixth by following the advice some hardly-able is likely to give you, to the effect that when you feel very strongly about a point, you shouldn't make it to the interviewer at all, you should turn and make it to the camera. The origin of this particularly hairy guideline is difficult to locate, but the end result of its implementation is startlingly unsatisfactory. Most television interviews operate on the unstated scenario that the interviewer and interviewee are talking to each other and the viewer is an eavesdropper who is doing no harm to nobody and cannot become directly involved. When the interviewee turns to address the camera and, through that camera, meets the eye of the viewer, it is deeply discomfiting to the viewer. Keep your eye on the interviewer and ignore where the cameras are. They are observers, not dancing partners.

Column Three of the grid should contain lots of questions. It should hold the questions the interviewer may have prepared in advance together with the questions which emerge logically from the points you have decided to make. For example, if you want to make claims about the safety-consciousness of your car-manufacturing company, you should expect that the interviewer will, in effect, say:

"Hang on. Car manufacturers have a terrible record for taking care of safety except when someone like Ralph Nadar makes a public stink about people dying as a result of manufacturing flaws. What's so different about your company?"

As you prepare the content of Column Three, be honest. Ask the questions the journalist would ask, not the questions you would like the journalist to ask. When you say that you're going to introduce air bags, the question you would like asked might be one of these.

"How many lives will that save each year?"

"Do you think the other manufacturers will follow your lead?"

If you think like a journalist, on the other hand, the questions you will ask include these.

"Air bags have been around for a long time. Why have you only got around to installing them *now*?"

"Ultimately, this will add to the cost of the car, won't it?"

"Why the timing of this announcement? We've never heard anything about safety from your company and now, when you're attacked by a consumer magazine, you come out with this?"

As Column Three fills up, close your eyes, run your finger along it, stop at random and ask aloud the question on which your digit has landed. Give it the best answer you can. If that answer includes one of the points you decided to make, deliver a small pat on your own back. If it does not include one of those points, add a bridge phrase and get it in. The process should be:

Answer + bridge + POINT

Bridges include phrases like:

"And..."

"But..."

"On the other hand..."

"It does seem, nevertheless, that..."

"It's worth pointing out, too..."

These particular examples are only that; examples. Do not learn them off by heart and apply them in all your interviews. One interviewee who regularly appears on a radio station near me constantly uses the bridging phrase "having said that, however, I must also..." Not only does this drive me, an uninvolved listener, berserk, but it also concentrates my mind, from the moment he is introduced as the next studio guest, on how soon and how often he'll come out with his pet phrase. As a result, my recall of what he has said in any interview is limited.

When Column Three has been filled and worked with, it is time to move briefly to Column Four. This is where you honestly put down the stinkers you hope you will never be asked, where you register the skeletons you hope to keep unclankingly concealed in the family or corporate closet. Everybody has a question they would rather not be asked. Many people have questions they would rather emigrate than have asked. The only problem is that if you concentrate on getting through the interview while fearful that this particular question may surface, you are trying to operate at two levels. If you have ever watched the child's party game where a kid is asked to make a circle in the air with its right hand and then a square in the air with its left hand and then do the two simultaneously, you will know that it is impossible. The human brain cannot handle two concerns at one time. So knowing that you have a problem for which you have no solution is likely to impair your capacity to communicate well.

Be honest. What is the question you truly dread about yourself, your company, your product or your service? Write it (or if you have a high anxiety level, write *them*) down in the last column. If you are a senior person in a large company, you are unlikely to find your colleagues or your internal PR people helpful. They tend to want to tell you what you should say, rather than speculate in a negative way about what might be asked of you.

When you have the stinker question or questions written

down, decide what you are going to say if they surface. This exercise can bring about a number of results. One company where I was consulting at the time changed its policy in one area as a result of the chief executive identifying as a possibility a nasty question about the company's performance in that area.

In another situation, it emerged that the problem had been solved in an overseas branch of the company and this solution could be quoted. One woman, preparing to represent her organisation, first noted down "People are ALWAYS muttering this about us," she said resentfully. "What they don't understand is that we have no choice. We HAVE to do it that way, because..."

When she ground to a halt two minutes later, all of her colleagues were beaming and rather hoping that the question would be asked so that she would have the opportunity to clear the air.

"Very dangerous," I commented. "You cannot afford to rely on being asked the right question. If that answer is important, get the point made even if you don't get asked the question."

Every now and again, there is a considerably more negative end result to this exercise. The interviewee knows what he or she is going to say, if asked the question, but hope springs eternal that the question will not be asked. That's fine. An answer may not be perfect, but it is the best you can come up with and if you have faced up to the problem and have the best available answer readily accessible to you, you can then concentrate on all of the other positive elements you can inject into the interview.

Be wary, though, of the Good Ship Lollipop approach to public communication. Many clients who come to my company seeking to prepare for TV or radio interviews want to peddle exclusively good news. They want to be on the sunny side of the street with a little halo on, having their picture taken as they raise the Little Match Girl to her feet. They are fearful of any negative question and twice as fearful of any negative content squeezing into any answer.

This is an unrealistic and unproductive stance. The ever-smiling prattler of generally-accepted platitudes who always wants to look on the bright side, spot the light at the end of the tunnel and pay attention to the silver lining around every cloud is a world-class pain in the ass, in media terms. The public management of bad news is much better PR than the constant effort to push the audience into ignoring the bad news and taking a better attitude to whatever minuscule good news is around. Being a great communicator, developing a good personal image, or creating a solid public perception for your organisation is not a matter of sending out press releases about new awards you have dreamed up or giving a smiling answer to every question. People want realism and content and honesty.

The fear of being asked negative questions always hangs over newcomers to radio and television. It should not be so. The more negative a question is, the more it is infused with hostility or outrage, the more likely it is to create attention and interest within the audience. A bland question invites people to lose interest. A question which invites the interviewee to explain how wonderful he is invites the audience to lose belief AND interest. A stinker creates the desire to listen and hear how the person queried copes with this difficult proposition.

When you are going on radio or television, then, do not get worried about the questions. You will judge yourself a success or a failure not because of the questions you are asked but because of the answers you give. The one thing you must do is answer the QUESTION, not answer the EMOTION. If you're a teenager, coming in later than you should, and your mother encounters you on the stairs and asks the question "Where were you until this hour?" you can answer the emotion in the question by getting emotional and suggesting that it's time she let you grow up and minded her own business and nobody on your road at your age has to answer questions like that. All of which leads to a brisk exchange of prejudices and a rapid grounding of one lippy teenager. Or you can answer the question straightforwardly. "I was down in Mikey's and we stopped at the corner shop on the way home." If you answer the question straightforwardly, as opposed to inferring its emotional tone, you are likely to get much further in opening a two-way communication: "…we stopped at the corner shop on the way home, and you know who was there? Do you remember the Regans who left for Australia? Well, the father has come back and he was telling me…"?

One of the best examples of this principle of answering the question, rather than the emotional tone of the question, happened to one industrialist who had, unexpectedly, closed down one of his plants. The tone of the interviewer reflected the public reaction, which was that the closure was, in itself, an example of poor judgement and short-term thinking, and that the way in which it had been done was inhuman. This was how the opening question ended:

"…and so you gave your managers eight hours notice that you were closing the plant. Eight *hours*!"

"In fact, I only gave them six hours," the industrialist said, with unexpected honesty and great calm." And the reason was simple. If I had…"

He went on to explain the wider implications of the closure and the interview continued. It was a difficult wicket to play, and many people, after the interview, still felt that the move had lacked judgement and human concern. But the industrialist had not added to his problems by outbursts of defensive self-righteousness. He had stayed with the facts, even when the facts did not seem to serve his interests.

In the next chapter, we will look at the different kinds of programmes or programme inserts, on both radio and TV, which may require your participation. The essentials of good media communication stay the same, however, no matter what shape is taken by a particular programme. They are:

A Good Brief
A good brief results from asking enough questions to ensure that when you get into the studio, you are able to deliver a good performance, as opposed to merely surviving a series of unpleasant surprises.

A Clear Decision

You should never go on a television or radio programme with your mind half made up. If you are going to appear, commit yourself to a wholehearted presence. Having a mental back door open ("Well, I'm not sure such serious issues should be discussed on TV at all...") is a pointless distraction. If you say "yes" to the invitation, mean it and act on it.

Preparation

With adequate preparation using the Preparation Grid, nasty shocks are prevented. In 20 years of training people to prepare them for television appearances, my company's tutors have *never* failed to predict the key questions which were eventually asked. We have never tried to predict the wording of those questions, but the main thrust of each was foreseen and planned for. If you prepare in realistic detail, no interviewer should be an object of terror.

Fair Play on Both Sides

It is not fair play for you to go on and use tricks to avoid answering fair questions. It is not fair for you to go on, determined merely to filibuster, talking for the sake of filling air time.

Similarly, it is not fair play for a production team to invite you on the basis of one briefing and then spring a quite different reality on you. 99.9 times out of a hundred, this won't happen, but someone you know always knows of the instance where it *did* happen to a friend of theirs. If, before you go on the air you find the goalposts have been moved in a way you know you cannot cope with, and you suspect that this is why they have been moved, don't go on, and explain in reasonable tones why you won't go on. You will cause them major problems by baulking a few moments before a live programme, but it wasn't you who moved the goalposts. If the goalposts are moved in mid-programme, go slow. Go slower. Think. And if you feel strongly enough, say so and leave. Nobody will talk about anything else for weeks.

However, it should be stressed that the number of times production teams go outside the ethics of their profession are few. Very few. Too few to plan or worry about in advance. You concentrate on your task and let them concentrate on theirs. We, the audience at home, with luck will find the end results of your separate efforts entertaining, informative or stimulating.

Chapter 7

Programme Slots and Interviewers' Styles

Television is the first truly democratic culture—the first culture available to everybody and entirely governed by what the people want. The most terrifying thing is what the people want

Clive Barnes

When you agree to go on a radio or TV programme, you appearance is generally in one of the following slots or programme types:

- Vox Pop Interviews

- News Bulletin Interviews

- Current Affairs Programme Interviews

- Chat Shows

- Personality Profile Interviews

- Quizes and Game Shows

Although the basic preparation facilitated by the grid is nearly always beneficial, there are factors to be taken into consideration in each case, if you plan to make the most of the very different opportunities they provide.

Vox Pop Interviews

The only time you do not lose marks for lack of preparation is if you appear on TV in a Vox Pop interview. Vox Pop is bowdlerised Latin meaning the Voice of the People, and this type of interview is used by programmers to establish a reaction among the general public to some piece of news, or to set a number of viewpoints in position before a public figure is interviewed about some topical matter. Vox Pop interviews may run for two or three minutes, with each interviewee speaking for perhaps 10 seconds. They are usually recorded in the open air in a busy street, although it sometimes happens that the story determines that location. A group of us were doing some training in the US last year and one tutor went home a day before the rest of us. That night we turned on our CNN news bulletin, and up he popped in a Vox Pop interview recorded at the airport. The reason was that the airlines had introduced new rules about the size and weight of carry-on luggage, and so it only made sense to record the reaction of air travellers in the location where you would expect to encounter air travellers in some numbers.

If you are approached by a mike-wielding interviewer on the street, you have three choices. You can:

- Smile, shake your head silently and keep going.

- Answer the question off the top of your head.

- Ask the interviewer to put his question, take a couple of seconds to think about the answer, and ask him to put the query again with the camera rolling.

News Bulletin Interviews

When your interview appears in the peak news bulletin on radio or TV, it may last for thirty seconds. That is, if your subject is riveting and brand new, and you, as a speaker, are vivid, urgent and get it all together in one answer without the interviewer having to ask you six supplementaries. It is much more likely, however, that the interview segment which is actually broadcast will be shorter than 20 seconds. This is because TV and radio are ruled by brevity. If you took all of the words spoken in a half hour television news programme and printed them, you wouldn't get enough to fill the front page of a broadsheet newspaper. You might not even get enough to fill page 1 of a tabloid. Television news is short, fast and to the point, and your interview needs to be the same.

There are two ways of gathering this kind of insert, one of them prevalent in the US, one more customary on this side of the Atlantic.

Imagine that the news item is a conference of widows demanding better income tax deals. The News wants an item.

In Europe
The interviewer comes along, picks out someone appropriate, whether that's the keynote speaker or the head of the Association, gets the video taperecorder rolling, and interviews the woman for anything between five and fifteen minutes. The interviewer takes the tape back to the studio, looks at it several times as he writes his story (which may, on the air, take 40 seconds to articulate) and picks out the answer which will serve best as a stand-alone. This is the answer which makes the best topical statement, or tells the simplest version of the essential story. If the interviewee subsequently feels hurt that the rest of the interview was cut out, she is being unrealistic. It doesn't mean that the rest was no good. It just meant that this bit met the programme needs best.

In the US
The interviewer goes along and gets the facts he wants to include in his story. With that story mentally written, he picks out his interviewee and does a preparatory chat.

"I'm going to ask you X," he'll say. "And I want you to cover X and Y in your answer. Can you do that? Let's do a dry run, shall we?"

The dry run, which goes on while the technicians are setting up, establishes if the interviewee can cover all the vital details in the time allowed. If she's waffling, she'll be told about it and given some help to get it together. Then the machinery is switched on, the interviewer asks his question, gets his answer, and knows that editing and viewing time back at the studios will be kept to a minimum.

I believe that the US style of news interviewing will take over from the traditional European style as more news material is fed live on the air into programmes. If a reporter is out in the field and knows he has one coherent answer on tape, he is much more comfortable leading into that answer and pressing the button than he is trying to cut into a much longer recording and cut out of it again when it is time to hand back to the people in the headquarters studio. Many of today's TV/radio reporters are reluctant to try it, because they do not trust interviewees to handle the ruthless demand: "Be good in 20 seconds or buzz off." It is arguable that a) more people can be good for 20 seconds than can be good for 7 minutes, and b) fewer people will subsequently see that slot broadcast, as opposed to the scenario which sees them interviewed at flattering length and later not only chopped into a miniature, but too often chopped so brusquely that what is broadcast ends on an upward inflection and leaves the audience with the impression that the interviewer suddenly clapped a hand over the interviewee's moving mouth.

No matter which way a news bulletin interview is done, the bottom line is that what appears in the programme will be very short. But it will be very useful. It is high profile. Think about a news bulletin. The newscaster tells a bit of the story, or a reporter does so. Then it's CUT, while the voice continues to be heard, and the first face to be seen is yours. The newscaster shuts up and local sound takes over your voice.

If it's TV, they can see you in full glorious colour. If it's radio, they can hear what you have to say without even the distraction of looking at you. (Quite often, the same recording serves for both radio and TV.) You, the audience at home, the reporter and the producer have one interest in common: that you will give a clear and comprehensive answer. The production team will have the unspoken hope that you are one of those rare people who can be fluently concise in news story-telling.

"You just wind him up and he goes," they will say about someone, and for that someone it is high praise from pressured professionals.

That does not mean a great rambling diatribe. It does mean making at least one worthwhile point before you entreat another question from the interviewer. Say everything you have to say without depending on the interviewer to cue you in.

If Mr Blank, being interviewed about an outbreak of industrial action, says simply that it is designed to show solidarity with the men in the railroad industry and then stops dead, he may do so in the hope of being asked why his men feel solidarity with the railroad workers. The interviewer, being independently-minded, may ask what good Mr Blank thinks the picket will do, thus removing Blank decisively from the position where he could make his point. Remember that the news interviewer is looking for the best possible interview, not a yes-and-no job. He is happy for you to get the facts (as you see them) across. However, beware of putting words in the interviewer's mouth. *Never* tell an interviewer what should be asked. Find a way to say what is on your mind without crossing into the interviewer's territory. Stay, as it were, on your own side of the net.

While you are listening to the questions, do so quietly and without nods and grunts. You do not know how long the question is going to be, and if you start nodding at the beginning of what turns out to be a lengthy preamble, you end up looking like one of those dogs people put in the back windows of their cars.

If you don't follow the question, stop the recording and seek clarification. If, on the other hand, the question is simply ambiguous, or shows that the interviewer does not quite understand your area of expertise, the most professional way to handle the question is to preface your answer with something like "If I understand you to mean X ..." This makes it clear to the audience (who may be as fogged as you are about the real meaning of the original question) that, while you are confused, you are not going to waste good air-time squabbling about it, and it also gives the interviewer the chance to set you right if you have chosen the wrong interpretation.

If you need to, think. On radio, you may pause for up to three seconds (look at the second hand of a watch and see how much longer that is than you imagine). On television, you may pause, as long as you make it clear that you are thinking and that you will come through with something at the end of the pause, for as long as seven or eight seconds. Never be rushed, in a news interview, into a quick half-thought-out response. There is a great pressure to be an instant expert. Resist it. The momentary gratification of speedy response is as nothing compared to the misery a half-wrong answer can bring you in your work or your home.

(An odd advantage of pausing in a recorded interview, particularly at the beginning of a response, is that you may make life a lot easier for the video-editor, who hates people who start answering questions before the person asking the questions has shut up.)

The time limitations on a news interview mean ruthless self-pruning. Filling in all of the background and making clear all of the ramifications is just not on. Define your purpose before you go on. Mr Blank may want to point out that his men have not struck since 1954, that they are grossly underpaid, and that they are up to their knees in water eight hours a day. What they struck about in 1954 does not matter to that purpose. Nor does the impact of inflation on wages in that sector of industry. Nor does the colour of the water.

Directness works in news interviews. "That's not true," works better than "In the light of today's Government report, it would appear that some of these points have been somewhat overstated." People watching television news or listening to radio news are like the chicken in the farmyard who is separated from her food by a short length of fencing. The chicken always tries to get through the wire to the food, instead of going around it. In the same way, people watching television want to get directly at the information being disseminated, rather than be led to it by circuitous routes. A direct approach, backed up by careful selection of the material to be quoted, is ideal. Selection is all important. Many people come to all kinds of interviews, including those for news programmes, laden with every piece of information on which they can lay hands, and do not select in advance what is really important.

Woolly tentativeness is death in introducing your thoughts through a news interview. The great American lawyer and freethinker, Clarence Darrow, was always good for an exciting news interview on almost any subject. According to a contemporary, he "... expressed to newspapermen very strong views in respect of various public questions, such as the treatment of negroes and defence of criminals and in every case made strong pronouncements without qualifications."

Darrow was not insensitive to the nuances of meaning and belief surrounding the issues he talked about. He simply had the clarity of mind to choose in advance how to raise the topics.

"When you want to get anything before the public," he wrote, "you must decide what is the thing you wish to emphasise at the time, and then state it strongly, forcefully and without qualification, and your view will then attract public attention to the particular thing you wish to emphasise—it will be news. If you qualify your main point the thing you wish to emphasise loses its news value—it loses its impact."

There is one other matter to be considered. That is how you will communicate when you are saying nothing. In news interviews, and also in some current affairs interviews (see below) which are shot on location, there is only one camera, whereas in a studio there may be two or three. In a multi-camera set up, the director can simply have buttons pressed in order to switch from a picture of the interviewer to that of the interviewee. With one camera, there is not that freedom. What usually happens is that the camera is trained on the interviewee during the course of the interview, and the questioner is not filmed at all One of the production team makes notes of the endings of the questions and the beginnings of the answers.

What then happens is that the interviewee is asked to stay in place, while the camera is turned around and focused upon the questioner. He/she then asks the same questions all over again. The interviewee will have someone to talk to at the right eye-level. The camera operator may also film some "reaction shots" of the interviewer as he nods and frowns in response to the answers the interviewee already gave, which are now in the can. The two sets of shots are married up later on by the editor.

Current Affairs Programmes

These can vary greatly in length, so it may be best to start with the shortest, which, typically, is the morning radio programme starting at perhaps 7.30 and going on until 9 or 9.30. This programme is based on the day's news and is made up of interviews lasting anywhere from three to five minutes. There is more time for the interviewee to expand and explain, but there is still no loose time for waffle. It is a great listening time for the "decision-makers," who tend to turn on the radio in their cars as they go to work in order to get a digest of the news and a survey of the emerging issues before they get to their desks. It is a great listening time; ergo, it is good exposition time. Depending on the newsiness of the item which provokes an invitation to you, the production people may telephone you the previous night or may find your number and reach you at 6.30 in the morning. If they ring you at 6.30 and offer you a choice of being interviewed on the telephone or going into studio, go into studio. Getting out of bed, taking a shower, preparing your grid and driving to the studios will get the adrenalin flowing and the mind functioning. (The time taken for all of this may also result in your interview happening between 8 and 9, rather than earlier. There are more people awake and listening during this later segment.)

Even if you agree, for logistical reasons, to take a telephone call, make sure that you have enough time to think and plan what you are going to say. Don't allow them to wake you and put you on the air before you have worked out whether it's Christmas or Tuesday. Telephone call interviews are both easier and more difficult than face-to-face interviews.

Because the balancing of sound between the studio and an incoming line is so difficult, the interviewer, wishing to save his sound operator's sanity, would be eager to minimise his questions to you, so he is marginally less likely to cut across you than he is in studio. Don't push your luck. If you are filling the airwaves with blown up blobs of nothing, he will cut across you pretty damn quick and to hell with dips in sound quality. Telephone interviews are difficult because you cannot see the person to whom you are talking. Make sure everybody in your house or office knows you're on air, so that you are not interrupted in person or on the line. Get into a room on your own and close your eyes to minimise distractions. Turn off the radio as soon as you hear the introduction to the item otherwise you will cause a nasty sound problem called *Howlaround.*

If you are invited onto one of the current affairs TV programmes, then it may be an interview with you on your own or a discussion where you are one of a number of people giving their views on a particular topic or news item. Either way, the preparation is the same. However, when more than one person is being interviewed, or when some of the speakers are setting out to disagree with you, the chemistry is somewhat different. You have an extra task. You must control your communication when you are not saying anything. Some people go on current affairs programmes with the fixed notion that the programme only matters when they are talking. So speaker A gets his innings, and speaker B gets launched. Speaker B is not actually attacking speaker A, and bored, he looks around him, observes what the cameras are doing and where the floor manager is. If a camera happens to catch him at it, he looks both discourteous and shifty. The rule is simple. You are interested in whatever ANYBODY is saying at the time they're saying it. Look at them, and don't, if a series of quick questions are put, look back and forth between interviewer and speaker so rapidly that you look like a spectator at Wimbledon.

On the other hand, if someone on the programme is going on at great length and telling outrageous lies about you, your company or your political party, you can either interrupt to call a halt to it, or you can react physically. It doesn't have to be a great theatrical head-shaking; if you indicate disbelief with even a raised eyebrow or a minor shrug, a good camera operator will catch it and a good director will cut to it. Briefly. But that's all you need. A picture is worth how many words? If someone's long verbiage is undercut by a sceptical facial reaction, the viewers at home make all sorts of useful judgements and hear relatively little of what immediately follows. So, even when you're not talking, you are communicating. Make sure you're communicating what you *planned* to communicate.

Whatever you do, having agreed to take part in a current affairs programme:

Don't announce on the air that the whole story is trivial and not worth talking about. If you do not want to talk, don't go on.

Don't waste time with phrases like "only my personal opinion, for what it's worth." We know you're not there to ghost for the Grand Vizier of Hyderabad, so we can assume the opinion is your own. And we will assess its worth with or without your permission.

Don't weaken what you are saying by announcing your generalisations as you come to them. "Well of course, it is a generalisation to say that all little boys like to play football, but I have to say it all the same..."

Don't try to cushion what you are saying with a fuzz of introductory, lets-put-this-thing-in-context remarks. People will switch channels.

Chat Shows
The received wisdom, a few years ago, was that chat shows were on the way out. Moribund. Dated. No part to play in the bright shimmering future of television.

What rescued chat shows from oblivion was the changeover from a general setting presided over by a pleasant personality to a thematic experience managed by a presenter who is much less a chairperson, much more an individual to be identified with or hated. The ones which have emerged are:

• In Britain, Terry Wogan going for a sweetly cynical lightness of touch distinguished by recurring in-phrases.

• Also in Britain, but meeting the needs of a very different market and age group, the presenter Jonathan Ross whose show seeks off-the-wall guests who would never have made it on to the more respectable shows, and whose style is a self-conscious parody of traditional chat show hosting.

• In Ireland, shows like *Bibi,* presented by Bibi Baskin, taking a thematic approach: let's look at women in business this week, and invite on women who have made it, women who have not made it, women with views, etc.

• In the US (and imported into Europe) Phil Donaghue's relentlessly energetic sustained interviews involving an audience pursued in person, row by row, by an earnest presenter pushing a microphone.

• Also in the US (and on the export market) Oprah Winfrey explores the intimate and invasive dressed in drop-dead clothes with an attitude to match.

In a sense, what has happened to chat shows is a form of niche-marketing. It's brand naming, and seeking to establish consumer loyalty, preferably among younger bit spenders. You are a Phil Donaghue person or a Terry Wogan person. You watch, not because of the guests, but because of the style, the process and the manner in which this particular programme or presenter attacks issues.

Two chat show hosts have survived all of the changes in direction, because they were brand names from early on.

In America, if you are a Johnny Carson person, you get into bed and turn on the television to enjoy him doing precisely what he has been doing for decades: starting with a rambling comedy monologue with "ad libs" directed to Ed McMahon or his orchestra, moving on to a series of famous guests who talk at his desk until the audience show the early signs of restiveness, at which stage he calls for an ad break and you go get yourself a cup of coffee or a beer.

In Ireland, people watch *The Late Late Show* (now exported in edited form to Britain) for the opposite reason. You watch Carson because you know exactly what he's going to do. You watch Byrne because you're never sure what he's going to do. He may suddenly do something out on location when you're expecting to see him in studio. He may attack a guest you expected him to flatter. He may get sentimental when you expected him to get shirty. He may cut off in her prime a telephone caller who could have delivered him four free minutes of controversy.

It is safe to predict that the chat show will always be with us, if for no other reason than that it is a relatively cheap broadcasting format. Some of the most famous guests come on a prime time programme free, gratis and for nothing, because they are plugging a movie or a book. Television lives off the printed word and—paradoxically—helps the printed word to survive. In the old days, the slogan was "You've read the book now see the movie." Today, the replacement slogan might be "You've seen the chat show, now read the book." A good innings on a popular show can push a book into the bestseller lists overnight, and that is true all over the Western world.

When you agree to go on a chat show, it is much more than an interview you are committed to. The equation is not you on one side and an interviewer on the other. You are on one side, and (depending on the particular show) the other side may include a live audience, at least some of which can be made up of people invited because it is likely they will disagree with what you're going to say, a panel of speakers, there either to discuss your subject with you, or because they are appearing as guests in their own right and may be brought into a discussion of your subject despite their lack of previous involvement or current fervour. In addition, there is an increasing trend to take live phone calls, which means that someone who does not have to identify themselves can make an input to the programme while the guest has to sit and (it happens) hear himself vilified by an unseen someone while the camera, baulked of a picture of the telephone caller, alternates between close ups of the attacked panellist and wandering reaction shots of the audience.

When you are invited to appear on a chat show, or in some cases before an invitation is extended, a researcher from the show will come and spend some time talking to you. The purpose of this visit it twofold. The researcher is a scout, sent out to get advance intelligence on the guest. Is the guest going to be a good talker or a lemon? Will the guest stand up to pressure or get defensive and pompous? Can the guest think quickly or is he that television nightmare, a man who needs to close his eyes for 5 seconds at the beginning of every sentence? Has the guest a sense of humour? Does the guest speak English, or if English is not their mother tongue, will they be able to handle an interview which is speedy and colloquial? Is the guest going to cover the same ground covered by a guest from a similar background a few weeks before? Has the guest something new to say?

The researcher is NOT there simply to make a few shorthand notes as cues for the presenter. The researcher is there to make preliminary judgements which will be supported or over-ridden by the rest of the production team back at the planning office, so it is a profound error to treat a researcher with condescension or with impatience. You may believe that, on the programme, you will be a riot in terms of humour, a revolution in terms of fresh ideas, a statesman in terms of oratory and an atomic bomb in terms of creating controversy. The researcher needs the evidence to bring back to the programme. If you simply touch on all of the areas in which you believe you will be competent, but do not share your actual competence with the researcher, you have only yourself to blame if the researcher develops a case of CYA (Cover Your Ass) and warns the presenter or producer that their prospective guest may not be the boon they assume he or she will be. Treat the session with the researcher as a rehearsal and give the researcher samples of the goodies you will dole out during your actual appearance.

The second function the researcher fulfils is that of a filter.

Most people, faced with a chat show researcher, press their personal "play" button. They assume, correctly, that the researcher wants them to talk. They do not realise that the researcher can also talk and may, indeed, be communicating very important messages throughout the conversation. The researcher may be indicating by body language alone and without any great intent to pass judgement, that when you talk about Z subject you are a delight, but once you get on to X you are a boring old pedant. The researcher may relish a particular joke or story, and by giving you a warm response, will hope that you get the message; tell that story or that joke on the air. The researcher may ask you a great many questions on a particular area and be self-evidently delighted with what emerges; the moral is that you must get to the material evoked by all those questions without making the presenter work so hard on the big night.

If the decision is made to have you on the show the researcher is likely to keep in touch with you. Keep asking questions about other guests, duration of items, topics to be covered. If at all possible, get hold of books written by other guests so that you can contribute, if they want you to contribute, on more than your own subject. Too many guests on chat shows suffer from monumental self-absorption. ("We've talked long enough about me—tell me, what did YOU think of my performance?") Chat show production teams have grown to expect this and they see it as a welcome surprise when a guest indicates an interest in helping the *whole* show to do well, and a willingness to prepare more than their own self-serving spiel.

Content is as important on a chat show as on a current affairs programme. Some of the issues which have changed the way society thinks and lives in the latter years of the twentieth century were first aired on chat shows, and were aired with time, respect and in sufficient detail to make people think. Therefore, preparation with the grid is as relevant if you are going on *The Late Late Show* or the *Phil Donaghue Show* as if you are going on *Today Tonight* or *Panorama*. Indeed, it may be more relevant. Because chat show hosts have so many guests to interview each week and so many items to introduce, they do not all have the chance to read, *in toto*, all of the books on which they will interview writer-guests. During a media tour of the United States, I found myself in Make Up beside a best selling author of police procedurals. I immediately began to ask him about particular characters and locations in his books. Details, anecdotes and explanations flew. The next moment, a production assistant appeared in the doorway and beckoned the author, indicating he would be on the programme in a matter of moments. The author, who was on a promotional tour so intense that it was unlikely he knew what city he was in, obviously did not know who the presenter of the show was.

"Oh," he said disappointedly to me. "You're not interviewing me, then?"

I shook my head.

"Hell," he said, "I thought I'd happened on a host who had actually read one of my books. I've been on 23 talk shows over the last three weeks, and not one of the hosts had read my new book. Jeez."

The author slouched out of the door and resentfully followed the PA. Within minutes he appeared on the overhead monitor, and he was a different man. No slouch. No resentment. He had a wealth of stories and added value, and as I watched him I was certain that he had read his new book again recently to remind himself of the story which he had probably finished a year before, had picked out the most interesting bits of it, and was determined to find his way to those bits, with or without helpful questions.

If you have written something and you think there is a possibility you will be interviewed by someone who has, at best, read a summary of it, resentment sets in in advance. Damn it all, they SHOULD have read it, shouldn't they? There ought to be a law, right?

Wrong. Keep in mind the old story about the farmer whose tractor broke down. He was in the middle of an important job, and so he climbed over the fence and went to see his next door neighbour through the neighbour's field towards the farmhouse, he was thinking about the timing of his request. The neighbour was likely to be busy at this time and in some need of his own tractor. The neighbour was a good man with machinery, and so the tractor was likely to be in very good mechanical order, but on the other hand, that might mean that the neighbour would not trust anybody else to handle his machine properly. The neighbour might not like the idea of two tractors appearing next door, when other people might not know one was broken and one only on loan. It might look as if the borrower was in fact doing much better than the lender...

The farmer had reached this point in his thinking when he knocked on the door and his smiling neighbour opened it.

"You know what you can do with your tractor?" the newcomer demanded. "You can shove it, that's what you can do with it!"

By the time some guests go on chat shows, they have reached a frame of mind not unlike that of the farmer with the broken down tractor. It is a frame of mind which is pointless. If the presenter has read your book, seen your film or witnessed your triumph, then the presenter can ask informed questions. If the presenter has not read your book, seen your film or witnessed your triumph, then the presenter can ask uninformed questions. It isn't the questions that will make it a great item, and turn you in to a TV personality. It's the answers.

There are, of course, other roles to be filled on chat shows. There is the court jester. The agent provocateur. If you are being asked to fulfil one of those roles, get a clear brief and prepare accordingly.

Radio chat shows are very much on the grow. They are a cheap and effective way of passing on information and of involving people in the discussion of topics of public relevance, whether they relate to advertising, consumerism, community affairs, legislation, environmentalism, sex, money or power.

The tendency is to have chat shows which are longer and which range over more than one topic, so that a host may be on the air for more than one hour (in the US, chat shows can last for three hours with the same presenter serving throughout.) The guests in studio can be supplemented by the playing of pre-recorded interviews, by the conducting of interviews with overseas figures of authority by phone, and by the taking of incoming phone calls. Handling incoming phone calls is an art form. Technically, it tends to be achieved by the donning of earphones. Simple? Not necessarily. Great soft heavy earphones on your head can be a trial, when they feed your own voice through to you so that it sounds strangely different to the voice you know and love. A question asked straightforwardly by a competent interviewer in studio is a lot easier to handle than the same question asked in a less coherent way by a caller whose natural nervousness is complicated by feeling strongly about the subject.

Many guests on radio phone-in chat shows make the mistake of listening to the question and immediately forgetting the questioner. Mrs White rings in to ask why the vans operated by your company spew such disgusting fumes, and you immediately turn to the compere and handle the matter without further reference to Mrs White. Not unexpectedly, this makes the disenfranchised Mrs White mad as hell, and when the compere goes back to her for a final comment, that comment is uncomplimentary to you and delivered with a fluent venom that takes strips off your skin. When Mrs White rings in with a query or complaint directed at you, the first thing to do is listen. Don't plan what you're going to say yet. With luck, you will already have identified her comment in advance on your grid, and will have the essential elements of a good answer to hand. So listen, and make notes. If she gives you the registration number of the van which particularly annoyed her, write it down. Write down her name. Do not rely on your memory. I once co-presented a programme with a young man who usually did the signing off at the end. Concluding one live edition, he said, with enormous bonhomie that until next week, it was time to say goodbye.

"So from Terry Prone and Me..."

A gargling noise suggested that he had forgotten his own name. I provided it and from then on the pad in front of him during a show always held my name and his at the bottom.

So Mrs White's name goes down in front of you, together with any easy-to-forget details. She finishes her question. You do not necessarily start answering immediately. You may need to clarify what she's asking you. You may need to put some questions to her.

If you do, use her name and ask them simply and respectfully. Once you are clear that you have the data on which to base a good solid answer, do so. If you do not have the information, get Mrs White's telephone number or tell the presenter that you will get the information and transmit it to the show so that they can put it out on air the next day.

Do not try to persuade Mrs White to agree with you. That is not your job. If she has an opposing viewpoint, that opposing viewpoint is made up of a confluence of facts, impressions and prejudices specific to her as an individual. It is an illusion fondly held by rational people that if you present the facts to people they will change their minds. They rarely do. People tend to listen to radio and TV programmes in quest of confirmation of their prejudices and largely reject material which challenges those prejudices. We all cherish our abilities as drivers and the openness of our minds. It's amazing that there are so many traffic accidents and so much irrationality about. The point I am making is that you are supposed to be communicating with the wider listening audience, not selling an idea to one unwilling potential purchaser. Use the question you are asked to get to the points you want to make, but do not pursue the caller in such a way as to invite a reiteration of earlier prejudicial views or to pressure her to recant on air.

Whatever you do in a phone in chat show, do not:

- Tell a caller he's a liar. You can indicate that this is the first time you've ever heard of an instance like the one he's talking about, but don't impugn his truthfulness.

- Tell a caller that he's in the pay of your competitor or, if it is a political phone in, that he is one of the Other Party. Deal with his question, remembering the advice to speakers going back to ancient Rome; argue to the subject, not to the man.

- Tell a caller that he is ignorant. If you can explain something in physics to me so that I can understand it, I am your friend for life. If you start the explanation by telling me I'm pig-ignorant about physics, I will silently hope both your legs rot.

- Get a name wrong. People like their own names. Habit, you know? Call me Treena and I am resentful ("I'm not well-known, so he doesn't feel he has to get my name right"), confused ("does he think he's talking to my cousin?") and cross.

Personality Profile Interviews

If you are not well known, do not read this section, because personality profile interviews tend, by their very nature, to be done with famous people. Every now and again some television professional will decide that ordinary people can be intriguing, too, and will set up a series of six half-hour interviews with people who are household names only in their own households. The resultant conversations can be fascinating, but they tend not to pull large audiences, because large audiences want to know more and more about fewer and fewer famous people. An old magazine editor for whom I worked at one point defined it for me.

"Do personality profiles for me," she instructed. "Famous people. Their likes and dislikes. Their successes and failures. Their triumphs and tragedies. Their funny stories and their feelings about their babies. Their illnesses—give me details, illness is always human interest stuff. Don't give me their goddam philosophies or their views on the current political situation in the Yemen. Tell me what they eat and what they wear in bed or don't wear in bed and what kind of bed they have."

Because the editor was massive in personality and power, I took fast notes and nodded a lot throughout this speech.

"And when I say famous, I mean famous," she added. "I

don't want people who paint pictures and people that think thoughts. I want people my readers are used to seeing onscreen. Big screen. Small screen. Maybe hearing on the radio. But otherwise, forget it."

For clarification, I asked if fame was, therefore, defined by television, films and to a lesser extent radio? I might bet on it, she told me. While I gaped, she added that she would consider a politician not because he might be a prime minister, but because he might be famous to ordinary readers through television appearances. People might, she allowed, be important, or influential, or authoritative or artistic, but if they were not known to her readers, then they were to be swiftly forgotten as prospects for a personality interview. Drawing a tentative bow at a venture, I names one of the best actors of the day.

"No."

She did not have to explain. This man was a stage performer, rarely if ever seen on TV, and usually seen in classic plays.

TV personality profiles are not quite so narrow in their catchment area, but they tend to be drawn from names known to the viewing public.

If you have been selected for this kind of programme, you have usually been interviewed before, so only the length and the degree of personal invasion may pose a challenge. Even though the subject is you, a degree of preparation is still a pre-requisite.

You should certainly have seen other editions of this particular programme before you agree to appear, in order to get a handle on the interviewer's style and the kind of areas within each person's biography he tends to focus on. In some cases, personality profiles are centred on a particular time or phase in someone's life. One series may look at Motherhood or Fatherhood, paying little attention to other aspects of the lifecycle. Another may examine the seminal changes in someone's life and the figures of influence who steered the subject towards one or another option. So be familiar with the playing field before you venture on to it.

To enhance your understanding, find out about why they have asked you to appear. Yes, you are famous. But which aspect of your fame do they want to focus on? Is it the legislation you brought in when you were in politics or the much more recent controversy your newspaper column provoked? Do they want to touch on your life as a husband-and-father or restrict the programme to an examination of your public role?

Once you have established the ground rules for the interview, you should prepare, this time using the grid not to make specific points, but to make sure that your life does not end up sounding like everybody else's life. I remember once interviewing a man about his school days and he said, as about half of the human race would say, that his school days were not very happy. When I asked him why, he managed to look both vague and hunted. Ten days after the interview was broadcast, we met by accident, and he told me that no illustration of why his school days should have been less than blissful occurred to him at the time when we were discussing those school days. Twenty four hours later, in his greenhouse, something reminded him of a schoolteacher he had regarded with blind terror for four years, having watched the school teacher torture some boys in his class.

"The school was in an old building that had been converted in a fairly half-hearted way," he told me. "For some reason, there were great pillars, about six of them, running up an aisle in our classroom. He would make the boys climb those pillars and cling half way up and then he would stick the nibs of pens into their bottoms. Again and again, he would do that, and they'd be crying and too afraid to slide down."

When I looked a little startled at this odd cruelty, the man telling me recalled example after example, with a sense of grievance mitigated not a whit by the fact that a good fifty five years had elapsed since his primary schooldays. What was sad about the whole thing was that his portrayal of that period as it emerged in the programme was a bromide soaked in watered milk, whereas it should have been a searing recollection with which thousands of adults, brutalised as children, would have identified.

When you are preparing for a personality profile interview,

put your own life on a brightly lit stage and find out which bits are the most interesting illustrations of how you became what you are today. Do not set out to be a sunshine-monger. Most of us learn more from our failures than from our successes, and are more interesting to people, especially if we are successful, when we are prepared to let others see our disasters. But, whether you talk about good times or bad, you must talk about them with vivid detail, you must illustrate rather than conceptualise, you must be anecdotal rather than dogmatic. If there are areas in your own life which have never been revealed and which would have bad implications for you if they were opened up to the audience of a TV or radio programme, do not go on the programme with a vague hope that the interviewer's research has not brought him to that point. Decide what you are going to say if you are asked that question, or get an agreement from them in writing that you will not be asked that question. I disapprove of the latter but some programmes based on the biographies of famous people (including *This is Your Life*) seem quite prepared to tell the life story of Mr Personality from start to finish, with the single exception of deleting this man's entire first marriage, kids and bankruptcy. Presumably the production people come to an agreement with the personality or those representing him that biographical amnesia will set in at a particular stage.

From your point of view, the objective must be a clear agreement about any topics or periods of your life that are out-of-bounds for the programme. If the production team will not agree to out-of-bounds areas, then they have an admirable sense of their duty to their customer, the viewer, but you may decide that such an interview would endanger your own position too much.

In preparing for a personality profile, remember that your life is not lived in isolation, and that the first-time negative revelations about parents may polarise your brothers and sisters and cause them to suffer considerable embarrassment, either in direct response to the programme or as a result of consequent press questioning. Think about the innocent by-standers before involving them in an unplanned way in a public fracas.

Quizes and Game Shows
Know the rules, get there on time and be prepared to make a felicitous fool of yourself.

Now that we have covered all of the preparation interviewees should undertake before appearing on radio or television, and since we have also looked at the requirements peculiar to different programme types, it is time to look briefly at interviewers and their styles. By rights, as a primer to media and public appearance survival, this book should not examine the habits of interviewers at all. However, long years of working with people before they make their first or second TV appearance has forced me to face up to the reality that many interviewees cannot concentrate on preparing themselves before they have slotted the interviewer into a mental box and been convinced that an interviewer's techniques and approach are not created on a once-off basis for the sole purpose of torturing the individual being interviewed.

Lifting the lid, therefore, on interviewer types, we find:

The Good Listener
He (please assume he/she to apply in the following) is the one who gazes into your eyes as you speak, and whose questions always link directly to your last remark. Probably the best interviewer of all, he is often under-rated because he spends no time enhancing his own image, and at the end of one of his interviews, many listeners will have forgotten his existence, although they will not have forgotten the content of the conversation. He has an unnerving habit of meeting inconsistencies in his interviewee with a courteous reminder of the interviewee's earlier words.

The Talker
He is not interested in hearing anybody's opinions other than his own, which are many, deeply held and often quite fascinating. He tends to ask lengthy questions which can be answered with a

"yes" or "no," and to have pet theories which he trots out in search of agreement from his interviewee. Some talkers are happy rural ramblers. Others are Current Affairs Experts. The latter produce questions like "Would you feel that the situation in Bechuanaland, which of course, closely parallels the tragic happenings in Cnunuba some two years ago, are due mainly to the actions of the minority Wu Wu group, who, as we know, are a more militant wing of the nationalist Trug party, or is it due to the right wing government of Major Binge?"

This is not an outrageous example. Betrand Russell, for instance, when interviewed by Malcolm Muggeridge on BBC in the fifties, met this opening question—

> My position is this—I consider that one of the major factors in reducing the world to its present rather melancholy condition has been the circumstance that human beings have been conditioned, for a variety of reasons, to believing that in some extraordinary way human life must or can, get better and better. Now I regard this as a complete fallacy. I don't think it gets better, nor indeed, do I think it gets worse. And I think the only way that human beings can live sanely in this world is by recognising that, and therefore I contend that the idea of progress has been a disintegrating idea, a fundamental error, and that there is very little hope for us until it's exploded.

It takes a brave and literate man to answer a "question" like that.

The Writer
He, like the flounder, has no confidence in his hearing or inventiveness. He does not listen to any answer he receives on the air, and so never bases a supplementary question on a previous response. His agenda is written out in advance, and is invariable. He will follow the order of his questions, even if it means bending the conversation double.

The answer to question 3 may have been included by the interviewee in the answer to 2 but 3 will get its innings nonetheless. Writers sometimes run out of questions before they run out of time, which is awkward. Contrariwise some equip themselves with so many that they could continue for days and it often sounds as if they have.

The Architect
Appearance is often more important to him than content. He has little pads covered with sketches of squares and circles, lays out scaffolding on which he proposes to build the interview, and divides it into mental time segments. Four and a half minutes for Life up to Adolescence, two minutes for Attempted Suicide, three minutes for Marriage, two and a half for Kids.

The Aggressor
Asks the most innocuous of questions as if unmasking a murderer. The aggressor satisfies the atavistic longing of the audience for A Good Row.

Many guests in television and radio studios focus on the personality of the interviewer. They forget their own duty to their material in wondering what the interviewer is up to. Author Brian Cleeve, in *Cry of Morning* has a scene in a TV studio where all the various participants are gazing at the presenter, projecting their hopes, fears, hates and aspirations on to him. And all of those projections, Cleeve points out, missed the point, because the presenter

> ...was committed to nothing, believed in nothing, except perhaps those shadows flickering on the monitor screens scattered about the huge chiaroscuro of the studio. Only those shadows, and even that belief had come to him by accident, by the chance of being offered this job that had become his life, that had suddenly and astonishingly fitted his soul like a glove sliding over a hand. Apart from that tenuous, professional belief there was inside him only an echoing, bottomless, emptiness that he himself was afraid of proving. Of finding that there was no end to it, that there was nothing, nothing, nothing there. Like the boy in the fable who could not shiver, could not feel fear, he

could not feel anything. Which was, perhaps, why he was
so good at television, why and how he understood the use
of silence.

That, in a nutshell, is the interviewer's job—the use of
silence.

Many, if not most broadcasters, whatever about the
idiosyncrasies of personal style which distinguish them from
each other, would subscribe to the code drawn up by Robin Day
for radio and TV interviewers:

1. The television interviewer must do his duty as a journalist,
   probing for facts and opinions.

2. He should set his own prejudices aside and put questions
   which reflect various opinions, disregarding probable
   accusations of bias.

3. He should not allow himself to be overawed in the presence
   of a powerful person.

4. He should not compromise the honesty of the interview by
   omitting awkward topics or by rigging questions in
   advance.

5. He should resist any inclination in those employing him to
   soften or rig an interview so as to secure a "prestige"
   appearance, or to please Authority; if after making his
   protest the interviewer feels he cannot honestly accept the
   arrangements, he should withdraw.

6. He should not submit his questions in advance* but it is
   reasonable to state the main areas of questioning. If he
   submits specific questions beforehand he is powerless to
   put any supplementary questions which may be vitally
   needed to clarify or challenge an answer.

7. He should give fair opportunity to answer questions,
   subject to the time-limits imposed by television.

8. He should never take advantage of his professional

experience to trap or embarrass someone unused to television appearances.

9. He should press his questions firmly and persistently, but not tediously, offensively, or merely in order to sound tough.

10. He should remember that a television interviewer is not employed as a debater, prosecutor, inquisitor, psychiatrist or third-degree expert, but as a journalist seeking information on behalf of the viewer.

(R. Day. *Television —A Personal Report.*)

* An exception is the non-controversial interview, i.e. factual questions to an expert when the programme demands compact answers for information only.

Having done a bit of stereotyping in one direction, how about devoting some moments to stereotyping (with the anonymous help of my TV and radio interviewer friends) the worst of the interviewees. Lift the lid there and this is what you may find.

Menace Interviewee/The Context Menace
This is the speaker who cannot address himself simply and vividly to the subject in hand, but goes back through history to set the scene. He can neither be side-tracked nor speeded up, and often has mannerisms like saying "Nineteen hundred and forty six," where the rest of us would say "the forties." If you cannot talk about a subject without giving a history lesson, do not go on.

Menace Interviewee/The Paranoia Menace
Suspicious from the moment he enters the studio, he talks very slowly, in the belief that he can keep a watch on his words better that way. Shies nervously at every question, and examines it, sometimes out loud, for snide implications.

Menace Interviewee/The Bluffer
Often a politician, he is in the business of filling as much time as

possible with as little as possible.

Menace Interviewee/The Reader

He has written down all his answers to all possible questions, and turns over the pages noisily, making "I'll be there in just a moment, wait for me" noises. The interviewer is driven frantic trying to think of a question which will not have its answer ready on the jotter.

Menace Interviewee/The Trick Merchant

Someone told him to smile at the end of his sentences. So a dreadful rictus engages his features after four phrases, and recurs appallingly.

Someone else told him to say "That's a very good question," or "I'm glad you asked me that question" so he does, inappropriately. He has a whole arsenal of nasty pre-digested flatteries up his sleeve, and they all look dated and horrid.

How not to be a menace interviewee? Abide by a code, something like Robin Day's Interviewer's Code.

A Code For Interviewees

1. The interviewee will prepare himself for the experience by searching out relevant facts, figures and examples.

2. The interviewee will work on these until they are clear and interesting to ordinary people.

3. The interviewee will not allow himself/herself to be overawed by the interviewer.

4. The interviewee will approach the interview as an interview, not as a means of scoring off the interviewer or engaging in debate or plugging the firm employing him or its products.

5. The interviewee will accept that the interviewer has a different set of priorities and that these are as valid as the interviewee's.

6. The interviewee will answer as fully and honestly as possible, without waffling or shouting the interviewer down.

7. The interviewee will make a genuine effort to provide something new and interesting for the listeners/viewers.

8. The interviewee will not invite the interviewer to waste time by a) excessive chumminess, b) pointless fighting, c) asking the interviewer's opinion, or d) gratuitous compliments.

9. The interviewee will not make everybody uneasy by acting suspiciously. He/she will prepare in advance for obvious dirty questions. After that, he/she will behave as Mark Twain described the participants in a cat-hunting expedition—"You pretended you didn't see the cat, the cat did not see you, and that neither of you knew there was a brick in the vicinity."

Chapter Eight

Specialist Broadcasting

Nobody is on my side, nobody takes part with me: I am cruelly used, nobody feels for my poor nerves.

Jane Austen, *Pride and Prejudice*

Many professional people have a deep suspicion of the media in general and of television in particular. Mention the possibility of a television or radio appearance to them and they make like a sixtyish maiden aunt offered a fiver for her favours by a sailor. Not only that, but they show great hostility and contempt for members of their own profession who go public and make a good job of it.

"Oh, the bright boy off *Checkpoint*." they'll sneer. "Oh, the TV doc."

As if being able to talk intelligently about one's work in public somehow lessened one's ability to do that work.

From the media journalist's point of view, this is infuriating. You are trying to put together a programme on some social problem which really needs a responsible doctor's comment, and you ring one of them after another. (The same thing happens if you are after a lawyer, psychiatrist or social planner). They will all treat you as if you were asking them to pose naked in the centre-fold of the *Pornographers' Weekly*.

"I'm awfully sorry," the first will say insincerely. "But I'm very busy and I don't really have time for that sort of thing."

You can tell that he brackets appearing on TV with robbing

from an anaesthetised patient.

"I'm not interested in publicity,"another will say frigidly, as if you were an advertising agency touting for his business.

"I'd be delighted, but I would need to do some preparation," a third will point out, adding reprovingly, "This is a most important subject, you know. I wouldn't wish to say anything which might be misconstrued or not be up-to-date with the latest research."

They always seem to want more time than is reasonable or sensible. I remember at one stage trying to get together a programme on anorexia nervosa, about which, at the time, there were a lot of rampant fallacies. I got in touch with one of the men who is acknowledged to be expert in the area. He said he would agree to be interviewed, but he would have to read the latest edition of the British Medical Journal first. How long would that take, I asked with urgent politeness.

Six weeks, he said.

Six weeks?

Yes, he said self-importantly, he was a very busy man.

The result, of course, was that I interviewed someone measurably less expert in the field, who was willing to come along and able to give sensible answers to questions of interest to lay listeners.

Despite the fact that relatively few professional people are willing to be involved in radio or television interviews (or indeed make comments to newspapers on topical stories relating to their area of expertise) the same group invariably crib that the media "always go to the same men" or "encourage the self-publicists." In fact, the media people take the best they can get, and if it works, they come back.

Sometimes what they get is very good indeed. On BBC Radio 2, the *Jimmy Young Programme* has nurtured a series of experts, from paediatricians to lawyers, and from GPs to shopping correspondents. All manage to be both authoritative and entertaining without baby-talking their audience or doing an injustice to their topic. In Ireland RTE Radio One's *Gay Byrne Show* has done much the same thing, developing specialists who are willing and more important who are *able* to make their expertise available to an unseen mass audience. One of the best radio doctors ever to broadcast was discovered by the Gay Byrne team. Clear, concise, unfrivolous, unpompous, this man also had a rare capacity to time his answers so that if there was no more than forty seconds remaining in the programme, he could be relied upon to finish his answer ten seconds from the end, to allow the presenter to do his wind-up.

Experts who are prepared to come along and make an effort to translate their expertise into lay-person's terms are rare. There might be more of them if there was not the ever present problem within many professional hierarchies of the "head man." Oeser's law, quoted in *The Peter Prescription* says that "there is a tendency for the person in the most powerful position in an organisation to spend all his time serving on committees and signing letters."

And, possibly, being interviewed. Head men are often out of touch with the day-to-day realities of their science or organisation, yet they want to be seen as leading lights, and if they maintain a strangle-hold on the public appearance possibilities presented to the organisation, broadcasts full of solemn fat generalisations are the end result. Nobody ever tells the Head Man this, because the position is akin to the position of a Bishop—having become one you never again have to eat a bad dinner or hear the truth about yourself.

Men and women further down the chain of command may be less qualified, but they are often better suited to public appearances, if only because their student days are closer to memory, and they will recall how certain terms of the trade are not readily understandable, or recollect the vividness of a particularly good lecturer, and seek to emulate him/her.

One of the main problems faced by the professional who goes on television is coping with the post factum reaction. Colleagues (because TV/radio exposure brings out a fantastic bitch-quotient in friends and co-workers) will point out every error of point nought nought nought three five in the figures quoted. The general public, far from being permanently enlightened by the lapidary phrases used, will go on their ignorant way just as before. The critics will have watched an American soap opera that night. It is all a great let-down.

Douglas Stuart, the BBC's former foreign correspondent, tells a story in his book of recollections to illustrate this point. It was, he said, brought home to him in a conversation he had in Germany during the fifties with the Minister of the Interior in Berlin, Herr Schroeder, who was, in Stuart's view, a handsome, well build and confident man.

He suggested that he must have made a good impression on the German public through his appearances on television when the proceedings of the Bundestag were broadcast "live." Schroeder disagreed strongly, arguing in favour of bringing the televising of the Parliament in the Federal Republic to an early close. He recalled that he had been in Trier on a visit just after a three day televised debate in the Bundestag during which he had spoken several times, appearing on screen during peak viewing times each day. In Trier, he had gone to the barber, who, after a couple of snips, looked down at his important client to remark:

"Surely I've seen you before." Schroeder made no answer. "Yes," said the barber. "I've seen you before. Now, where was it?" He thought for a moment, and then, his face brightening as his scissors clicked, he announced to the whole room: "Of course, it was on the telly. I remember that I said to myself: there's a man with a fine head of hair and I'd like to cut it". The story made Schroeder very melancholy. "You see," he said to me, "Nobody listens on television. They only see what they want to see; the barber, a head of hair to cut, the tailor a well-cut or badly cut suit. The impression is what counts."

This is not quite true. Impression is certainly important. If you produce all of the facts in the world to support an argument on television, and are nonetheless perceived by the viewers as being unpleasant, your argument will be lost. But the "impression-is-all" rule often seems, in the days following a broadcast, to be quite literally true. Massive unjustified paranoia can result. A Senior Statesman who shall be nameless once came to me in a state of simmering resentment consequent on a TV appearance (his first, despite his relatively advanced age). Television was a rubbish medium, he told me.

I shoved a cup of coffee across the table to him and was glad the table was a big one. Being close to his rage could give you third degree burns, I figured.

Not only was television a rubbish medium, but the people who watched it watched it without discrimination or judgement, he told me. I proffered the sugar and he took four spoonfuls, which in the context, made sense.

He didn't agree with much that Karl Marx had said, he told me, stirring the coffee with such force that tidal waves of it overflowed into the saucer, but he was right to say that television was the opiate of the people. This seemed to me a somewhat freehand translation of what Marx had actually said, but I stayed silent while he tipped the coffee overflow back into his cup from the saucer. He used a paper napkin to mop up the saucer, and then, presumably on the basis that a balled up lump of damp paper had to be a tissue, shoved it in his pocket.

"Do you know what people said after I was on that programme? They said I had a granite jaw. What kind of nonsense is that? What kind of intelligence makes that kind of judgement after a man has spoken on the media?"

I gave an aw-shucks shrug. I couldn't tell him that his jaw made Mount Rushmore look like marshmallow. He drank his coffee with a vengeance and gazed at me with negative expectation, the patent implication of his gaze being that I was going to fight with him about the virtues of the television-viewing public.

"Why are you here?" I eventually asked.

"I want you to tell me why it happened and whether I should ever go on TV again or avoid it like pneumonic plague."

This took me aback, partly because one always assumes a plague is going to be Bubonic rather than pneumonic, and partly because of the sudden simple sense he was making. Out of his briefcase he produced a videotape of the programme on which he had appeared.

"Someone told me you never watch TV unless you have to,"

he told me approvingly. "So I brought along the tape in case you hadn't seen it."

In went the tape into the machine. On came the programme, jaw and all. It lasted fifteen minutes, and positioned my visitor between two other statesmen of similar age and stature. The presenter was a man of considerable academic background who reeked of books and concepts and philosophical constructs.

He hadn't so much moved the discussion along as stayed alongside it, favouring each of the participants in turn with a reverent nodding attention. When the programme finished, I suggested to my visitor that he might gamble with me.

"I'll wager you a fiver I can tell you what viewers said to that other speaker on your left," I said.

My visitor started to reach into his wallet pocket. I indicated that the bet would be hypothetical.

"They said he really looked the part," I postulated. "They said look at his beautiful silvery hair, wouldn't you think he was an ambassador? They said he's dressed beautifully, isn't it obvious he's a Senator?"

My visitor agreed that he had heard such comments, but added tersely that it was better than having A Jaw. And anyway, he added, getting mad all over again, didn't this whole thing prove the point he was making earlier that TV audiences were the pits and only saw superficial things? No, I said, taking my courage in one hand because there wasn't much of it. It proved that when performers on television said nothing worth listening to, viewers filled in the gaps by looking at, and thinking about, peripheral things, like buttons and badges and shirt-colours and habits and ties...

"And jaws," he concluded.

And jaws, I conceded. The point being that people can take on board information at a rate of about 300 words a minute, although most scripted reports on radio and television come in at about 140-150 words a minute. The pack on the videotaped programme had been about 120 words a minute. A tedious, meandering pace which had forced viewers to fill in the many attention gaps.

"But I had been TOLD to talk slowly," he said.

Not by the production team, I assumed.

"No, in the past, people listening to me have said I was difficult to follow because I talk quickly. They told me to slow down."

People who tell fast talkers to slow down should be shot. The fast talker still thinks at the same pace, so the words coming out of the mouth and the ideas coming out of the brain go out of sync.

The advice is *never* good, because although someone may be hard to follow, it is the choice of words, the linking of ideas and the illustration of those ideas which makes them difficult to follow, not the pace. Blind people listening to Talking Books for years complained that the normal pace of reading bored them rigid, because they could understand information at a much fast speed. The technical people went to work on the problem and came up with cassette players which could replay a take at almost double the normal speed without much distortion. Now, those tape recorders are available to the general public. I use mine whenever I have to listen to a radio programme I have missed. I can listen to an hour's programme on the maximum speed, fast-forwarding the machine through the commercial breaks, in about a half an hour, without missing anything—in fact, with arguably better recall than would result from the slower pace of the real thing, which tends to provide space in which to be distracted.

"What viewers saw was three slow-talking men being ponderous about nothing. The viewers who talked about your jaw mustn't have any other channel, because if they had, they'd have been gone to it."

My visitor was outraged by the allegation that he had talked about nothing.

"I covered X," he told me, "I reviewed Y."

Deadly words. Covered. Reviewed. The Expert examining what is not new. The Expert reiterating. Not the Expert discovering ideas for the viewing audience and with the same excitement he brought to those ideas and concepts when first encountering them. The programme amounted to up-market pub talk among specialists. After dinner waffle. It should be remembered that after dinner conversations, at their most stimulating, are often NOT between peers or people with a shared discipline. They are between people of contrasting experience, who seek to be interesting to each other.

"None of you, on that programme, set out to be interesting to anybody," I concluded. "You behaved as though your personal eminence gave you a licence to kill through boredom."

My visitor thought about that for a long time.

"You're saying it's not the viewers' fault?"

Right.

"You're saying I didn't take it seriously enough?"

Right.

"You're saying I could be good on TV if I approached it in a different way?"

Right.

For several months, the statesman worked in my company's studios, learning to prepare his material, and unlearning his contempt for the audience. Then he began to appear. Just a little at first. Then more often. That was three years ago. On the day I wrote this, a man commented to me about Mr Jaw's appearance on last night's prime time discussion programme.

"There's a natural," he told me. "There's a man who wouldn't need your kind of training."

I did a secret smile.

"What did you think of his jaw?" I asked.

"What do you mean, his jaw? Nothing wrong with his jaw? Jaw same as everybody else. But a talker—wow!"

Mr Jaw was an expert who was prepared to spend time coming to terms with the realities of television and the necessity to make old things new and new things familiar to the viewing audience. He is rare in that. He is also rare in his continuing willingness to put in preparation time before every single TV and radio appearance. He is truly exceptional in his willingness to serve an audience while no longer thinking dismissively of those viewing as a stupid mass.

Peter Ustinov holds that: "There is nothing more forbidding for the solitary viewer than to be addressed as though he were a huge cross-section of the populace."

When scientists and other knowledgeable figures think of their listeners as contemptible cross-sections, awful appearances result. We are individuals, out here. We are not stupid. If you talk clearly to us without jargon, we will understand you fine. If you talk with urgency and belief, we might, just possibly, end up following your advice.

It is the mistake of many people's lives that they ignore, are frightened by, or contemptuous of the media. Hubert Humphrey once admitted that the greatest mistake of his political life was not learning how to use television properly.

Selecting a series of sample "professions" to deal with in more detail here is difficult, because the essence of television and radio is topicality. Today may throw up an event which can bring into prominence a certain profession to which nobody has paid any attention up to now. The moon landings gave a mercifully short-lived innings to space "experts." Oil-well blow-outs make professionals like Red Adair into household names for a period. An air-crash in the middle of a holiday season may mean that invitations to talk in public start coming through to aviation experts and travel specialists.

What follows, then, is a selection of areas which, may serve as blue-prints for professions not covered in detail.

Doctors

Most doctors, when they approach a microphone, require that they be addressed simply as "doctor," with no name appended. (This is OK on radio, but always seems to me to be a bit silly on TV. If a doctor appears any way frequently, his/her identity gets around even if the name is not trumpeted.) This ruling comes from the various medical organisations.

Interviews

With the exception of those few (like the medics on British radio's Jimmy Young and Ireland's Gay Byrne programmes) who have what amounts to a medical column of the air on a regular basis, most doctors appear on programmes in reaction to some outside event.

There may be a major meeting of one or other of the medical associations, or an outbreak of some disease, and someone is required to give an expert opinion on it. (If there is a serious enough outbreak, of course, the Department of Health will appoint someone to act as spokesperson.)

Doctors as a group tend to be over-cautious when asked for topical comment. They will go to endless lengths to nominate someone else, sometimes because (as surveys show) some doctors are not sufficiently well up on the professional literature of their trade, and are becoming more dependent on glossy handouts from drug companies.

If and when they actually agree to go on radio or television, doctors as a rule have an unfortunate unwillingness to admit ignorance on any subject. If you are asked a question on radio or TV that you cannot answer, or should not answer, or do not feel safe in answering, say so. Doctors dislike admitting they do not know everything, and often cover up by saying that they would prefer not to be committed on such and such a point. "I don't know" is a better answer, because it is not liable to misinterpretation by the chronically anxious. They can take all kinds of negative meanings out of a doctor not wanting to be committed on some point.

On the other hand, protect yourself from your own inexperience. If, for example, you are asked to talk about an outbreak of rickets and you happen to practise in a wealthy, well-fed, non-rickety suburb, you may not be the right person, this time. Take a rain-check and suggest someone you think would be good in your stead.

Doctors should tell the truth. It sounds a truism, but many doctors assume, wrongly, that the public cannot take too much truthfulness. Some even have pet fatal diseases they do not want to admit kill anybody. I did an interview once with a doctor who was hell-bent on persuading people with a particular ailment to come for treatment. At once. Right away. In fact, yesterday. After the broadcast, I asked him what the cure consisted of, and what its success rate was. (Neither question had seemed relevant during the interview, although heaven knows why not, in retrospect.) The "cure" fixed up a half of one percent of sufferers. In that case, I said, why not leave the poor divils alone—aren't they going to die one way or the other.

"Oh," he said, horrified. "We can't give that kind of pessimistic impression."

It is the duty of the doctor making a public appearance to help people to deal with reality. Another medical story I dealt with some time back concerned one aspect of the physical damage done by very heavy drinking.

The medics concerned were very anxious not to say that the damage was considerable and virtually irreversible, as is the truth. It would only distress families of those who had been drinking heavily in the past, but who had stopped, they said. True. Except that soft-pedalling lessened the impact for people who might, at the time of the broadcast, be just embarking on a lifetime of booze. It also strangled the speakers. There they were, trying to indicate the importance of what they were on about, while not admitting its real importance—like playing tennis one-handed with a golf-club.

As for all interviewees it is advisable to work out, before you get to the studio, areas of likely discussion. If, for example, a doctor is going to talk about a radical change in medical opinion on some disease or treatment (an example topical over the past ten years has been the decline in the use of electro-convulsive therapy in mental illness) then it is logical that doctors as a group have not reached this apparently obvious conclusion before now? (Alex Comfort's *The Anxiety Makers* which deals with the panic peddling done by the medical hierarchy in past centuries is a convincing argument for the intrusion of the media into medicine. Anyone reading it will be convinced that if radio and television had been around sooner, the fallacies it records would have been scotched decades earlier, because reporters would have insisted on asking stupid, irrelevant, uneducated, sensational, intuitive questions which would have forced the doctors to think again).

If you are asked a "Has the medical profession stopped beating his wife?" question, then do not get defensive for the entire profession. Always concede a small point in the interests of making a bigger one, especially if the small point is really indefensible.

Remember, too, that a favourite gambit of interviewers the world over is "we have a great many mothers/commercial travellers/coal miners (depending on the topic under discussion) listening to this programme—if you could talk directly to them, what advice would you give?" Be prepared for it.

Preparation generally means standing a little outside the assumptions of your profession. Ask yourself the question the lay-person wants asked, even if your private opinion is that it is a wrong and irrelevant query. (Robin Day has been known to ask the milkman what he would like to ask the Prime Minister, before Day interviews the Premier. And furthermore, Day has used the milkman's question in the subsequent broadcast.)

If it does nothing else, this preparation cuts down the possibility of nasty surprises. Some time back, I interviewed a psychiatrist who was dealing with problems created by a certain kind of societal development. Very serious, these problems, he said. Going to get worse, he said. Didn't respond very well to medication he said.

Why then, I asked logically, was he not out protesting with a placard against the cause, instead of vainly trying to palliate the symptoms? He looked so totally blank and fell so totally dumb that I had to fill in the gap and close the interview. He said afterwards that he had simply not addressed himself to that possibility before, and that it robbed him of breath. Looking at his subject from the outside before he came into the studio would have turned that into a question he would have welcomed.

Preparation also means taking the jargon out of what you plan to say. There is no reason why medical descriptions cannot be put in clear layperson's terms, and every reason why they should be. As you drive to the studio, run over in your mind the terms you may need to use in discussion of the topic in hand. Can you give a quick homely definition for each? If the word-picture is effective and truthful, is there a strict necessity to use the technical term at all, except to impress your peers, who probably will not be listening anyway. Technical terms followed by definitions give a lecture flavour to the otherwise chatty conversation of an interview, and the fact is that any professional can only broadcast well to the general public if he puts his own colleagues and/or superiors out of mind first.

So—

Don't keep making disclaimers on the lines that this is only your opinion. Do it once. After that, we will accept that your views have not been sanctified by a general international meeting of your profession, and that there is a possibility that someone in Fiji may disagree with you. Get on.

Don't keep citing references. Radio and TV do not take well to footnotes. Assimilate and make your own of the facts and findings, and then tell the story as simply as you can. It is not a to-be-defined article in the *Lancet*.

Do, especially if you are giving a talk as opposed to taking part in a discussion or interview, keep before the listener's mind what is being talked about. There are cheerier experiences than coming into a room where a radio is playing and hearing a long, threatening medical talk which seems to suggest that all of your everyday symptoms presage madness, paralysis and death.

Do present a clear picture. If you qualify every statement as you go along ("This is, of course, only the general picture. Very often there are small differences in the presenting problem, etc etc.") you will confuse the listener who cannot go back to the beginning of the broadcast and remind himself/herself of your central theme.

If possible, take the smallest aspect of the subject that you can—hives, for instance, rather than allergies, and work up a larger picture pointillist-fashion with a series of smaller elements.

Ministers of Religion

Priests, nuns and ministers turn up in all kinds of programmes. For brevity's sake, we will deal with three: the discussion, the talk-to-camera and the televised religious service.

Not much needs to be said about discussion programmes that has not been said elsewhere in this book. Except perhaps, for one consideration. Ministers of religion are often asked onto discussion panels for the wrong reasons. Sometimes a programme which is centering on a particular local community issue will expect the priest or rector to want to be asked along as resident expert, as he sometimes does and is. Modesty and realism should dictate acceptance or polite refusal.

In the same way, priests are occasionally asked to appear because of a misinterpretation of the notion of broadcasting balance. ("We'll get a rabbi, a vicar and a priest".) The poor man has been chosen as a type, and may well find that it is virtually impossible to say anything except what the type seems to dictate. It is difficult to know this in advance, but asking for the right information, like who else is on the programme, what length is the item why is it on, and may help.

The talk-to-camera is an exceptionally difficult part of the television art or craft, and it is quite often undertaken without training by men who are called upon to fill those five minute "God Slots" the TV stations provide as a concession to the existence of God. That so many of the men who undertake the job are good at it is an indication that their belief in His existence may be well-founded.

Some, on the other hand, are awful banal, trivial, stagey, old-fashioned and coy, as underlined by the instant success in Ireland of a comedian named Dermot Morgan who created a sermonising priest named Fr Brian Trendy, whose spine-shivering tweeness rang a resounding bell among the watching public.

The "Ah, sure aren't we all in this Christianity business

together" posture adopted by some of the younger TV preachers is as unsuited to the medium as the straight-from-the-pulpit declarations of some of the older men. Neither deals with the reality of the TV audience, which is that they are not all the converted, and secondly, that they have been watching other programmes all night and still have the choice to switch over to something else if the "God Slot" is a bore.

The best talker-to-camera I have ever seen had this dilemma put very forcefully to him when he was embarking on his first series of "Epilogue" programmes in Northern Ireland. An older priest with a great deal of experience under his Roman collar, put it this way to him.

"The moment the red light goes on in the studio, and you're flashed onto the people's screens with 'Fr X, C.C.' written across your chest, there's going to be a Protestant down the Shankill Road who's going to say 'turn that effin' thing off, would ye?' That's the F point, and you have to be bloody good, you have to really grab his attention, before he'll let you past it. If you're really very good he'll keep you on to the end, and then he'll say 'What a load of s—t.' That's the S point, and if you reach it you're not doing badly."

That this kind of impatience is not limited to people of extreme religious views was highlighted for me recently when a mild tempered girlfriend very decidedly cut a priest off at the F point one evening when I was in her flat. He had begun his little spiel with a slow-paced rendition of the old nursery rhyme "Here's the Church, here's the steeple, look in the door and you'll see all the people." When he got to "steeple" she switched off.

"I believe in giving all those guys a chance," she said fair-mindedly, "but if he can't come up with better than that ..."

What this means is that the religious cannot afford to mess around in those first vital moments. Slow starters fail on television, because people will not sit and watch if their interest has not been wooed and won, as it is wooed and won by the expertly orchestrated advertisements and programmes they can watch on their various channels. A long look at the ads is a chastening experience. They are bright, they have got music, good looking people, and they grab the attention straight away. They have to. They cost a mint and they last thirty or forty seconds a time. So the introductory paragraphs that creep in when it comes to getting the talk-to camera down on paper should be let stand only for long enough to get the writing underway. Later, the writer should go back and honestly ask himself/herself "OK, where did I stop dancing-on-the-spot and really get going?" Everything prior to the getting going should be chopped off. The F point is not a moveable feast. It is there in the first thirty seconds. Always. The simple, the personal, the particular should always begin such a talk. Never the international, impersonal or general.

Example.

He lived quite near me. He was an old man. A blunt man. A plain blunt man who chewed and spat tobacco. He was a man who called a spade a spade, and if he was in bad humour he called it a lot more.

One day, as we were working together, he said to me, quite out of the blue "Tell me, then, why did he forgive them?" I said "Who?" And he said "God on the Cross." And he went on to point out in the plainest possible terms that he wouldn't have forgiven them under any circumstances if they'd nailed him to a cross. For him, the mystery of the Gospel wasn't the walking on the waters, or the raising of Lazarus, or even the resurrection from the dead, but why or how Christ could forgive his executioners.

The speaker then went on to deal with forgiveness in our daily lives, mentioning rows in families, disputes over wills and land, and ending up with a short paragraph about war. A less expert talker might have begun with a large statement about international conflicts.

In talking publicly, whether on television or from a platform, clergymen need to be wary of preacher's cliches. Most offensive of these is the use of Latinisms. "Possunt quia vindentur posse, Virgil said, and it's a motto we could all take to heart," says the priest.

What he has conveyed to the listener is "I was educated and I'm going to give you the benefit of my book learning."

Another preacher's cliche is the holy phrase. "And I reflected" and "My dear people," are signposts which say "This is familiar ground, folks, you've been here before. Feel free to switch off your mind".

The same message comes from the predictable inflection pattern which priests and ministers often develop. This usually takes the form of a dipping inflection at the end of each sentence, and the lack of sufficient light-and-shade within each paragraph. It can occasionally amount to a deadening speech "tune." Using a tape-recorder or asking someone to spot it and tell you, is the way to eliminate it.

Observation is very important in the business of interesting people in the ideas you want them to know about. Let's say your subject is children. If you can dredge up from your memory some little facet of children's lives which has not been done to death, then you may trigger other people's memories.

"That man really knows kids" is a compliment not far from "That man really knows me."

It is a skill and it is hard work developing it. Your quotations need to be deadly accurate—if they're not deadly accurate, they won't ring true to people who have kids. And there are a lot of them about.

Whatever you talk about, do not overload your script. Research at various universities, notably Leeds, has shown that listeners cannot remember more than about four points of any talk, however riveting. (You can test this at home—the results are very disconcerting.) More than four main points in a five minute talk will certainly confuse the listener and dissipate the impact. No points at all mean that you have wasted your time waffling on a central theme. The advantage of restricting your talk to three or four points is that notes become more concise and less important. Notes, in any case, can be a problem on television—there is a Morton's Fork thing about them. The only people who use them really well are the professionals, who are the only people who probably do not need to use them at all.

Teleprompters, or autocue machines are increasingly at the disposal of TV talkers-to-camera. Many are thrilled when they first see one. The autocue is, incidentally, a screen over the lens of a camera on to which the words the speaker wants to say are run. What people do not realise is that reading from an autocue tends to make even a talk written in beautiful spoken English sound stilted and "read". Many viewers too, are now sensitive to the side-to-side movements of the autocue reader's eyes.

Autocue is a mixed blessing. Newsreaders have developed a dependency of such magnitude on it that when it breaks down, they are thrown into visible disarray by having to do the old fashioned thing—read off a piece of paper and tell the camera what they have found on that piece of paper. On some stations, autocue is not provided for some of the smaller, late-evening bulletins. Signs on it. Those are the bulletins where you have a really good chance to get acquainted with the top of the newsreader's head and a doubt comes into your mind as to what kind of eyes the newsreader has, because that person on-screen is not doing the usual performance of looking you straight in the eye and telling you things. The person is in head down survival mode. It speaks volumes about the undesirability of dependence on autocue.

If you have to use autocue, find out about it well in advance, and seek training on it. The television production people are, unfortunately, likely to tell you that it's dead easy, you do not need any training; just send in your script for typing up on the autocue roll and all will be well.

All may NOT be well. A few examples.

The man who was flung in at the deep end of autocue and had nobody to advise him. Two years later, because individuals from the viewing audience kept coming to him and asking him why he was always looking down on them and not meeting their eye, he figured he needed some remedial training. It emerged that because of the positioning of the camera and the lights in the studio where he had started using autocue, there was a shiny bit at the top of the screen on which the words were due to appear. Because he was new to the game, he didn't know that this was easily solved, and so he compensated by reading the words in the bottom quarter of the screen. The end result, as picked up by the camera, was that instead of looking at the viewer straight in the face, instead of establishing what the Americans enthusiastically call "four eye contact," this man seemed to be obsessive about informing the viewer's navel. He talked to the belly-button of the home audience. He was serious with that navel. He was occasionally humorous with it. He told it the truth. Brought it the latest.

People watching his breakfasts didn't know what to make of them. They were not sure what it was he was doing, but they were sure that they had a semi-conscious desire to slide off their sittingroom couches onto the floor in the hope of meeting his eyes from a lower point. But no matter how low you crouched, he still ended up in a collusive relationship with your navel.

When he worked out what he was doing, remedy was simple. He had to learn to read from the top or middle of the screen instead of from the bottom. It was a simple remedy. That did not mean it was easy. When a golf pro shows you how to change your grip and your swing, it's simple. But after twenty years of a homegrown grip and swing, it is paralysingly difficult. For several weeks although the broadcaster managed to get his gaze line right, he did it at such a cost in concentration that viewers at home might have been forgiven for believing that he had got on fine with their navels but he truly HATED their faces.

When you get the chance to examine on-camera autocue (speechmaker's autocue will be dealt with in a later chapter) you will find that your script has been typed, in large format onto a roll of paper an inch or so narrower than a toilet roll. Typing, in order to fit well within the borders of this narrower-than-a-toilet-roll paper, has to be much more broken up than it would be if it were typed on A4 paper. So sentences you were used to seeing running uninterrupted across your own typed page may be broken up two or three times. This can be quite unnerving, so make sure you have enough time to get to know the script in its new shape. See if you can spot a typo in the text, and tell the operator about it. She will immediately get busy with a bottle of Tipp-Ex and a felt-tipped pen, and will hand-correct the roll while you watch. If you decide you need to cut a paragraph, she will get busy with a scissors and a stick of glue. Out will come the paragraph, and the bit of paper above where the physical cut happened will be stuck to the top of the bit of paper which followed it. All of which should make you aware of the marvellous flexibility of on-camera autocue. It can be changed up to the moment you are going on air. (In fact, in some cases, the latter half of an autocue script has been changed while a newsreader is going through the first half of the script on the air.) It should also make you aware of what an ally the autocue operator can be.

Some performers develop an absolute dependence on a particular autocue operator who has a particular empathy with the performer's pace of delivery. Autocue operators, the majority of whom are women, are a little like unseen accompanists; anybody playing the piano in support of a singer can get the notes right, but a great accompanist does immeasurably more than that, and a great autocue operator does a lot more than keep the script rolling up.

Indeed, presenter/producer Desmond Wilcox tells a story underlining just how central to a good performance an autocue operator may be. Wilcox was presenting a complex current affairs programme with many different elements coming together in such a tightly-paced way that the presenter, turning to his autocue camera, might be completely dependent upon the words appearing there to give him a clue as to what was coming next. Shortly before everybody moved into the studio to do that night's broadcast, Wilcox had a squabble with the autocue operator, who huffed off behind the cameras as the signature tune began to play. Wilcox got on with the task of presenting and interviewing. At the end of one particularly onerous interview, he turned with a sense of relief to the autocue, because he had no recollection of what the next item was. There were the words. Neat. Easy to read. But not totally familiar, because the autocue operator had handprinted them after the show had gone on the air.

"Blow me a kiss right now or I won't put up another word!" the screen told Wilcox.

His mind boggled. But it unboggled quickly enough for him to do a subtly disguised blown kiss (have you ever seen a subtly disguised blown kiss? Me neither) and the next paragraph rolled up in front of him in response to it. What the audience at home made of it is not recorded. Presumably they watched him to see if he was harbouring a nervous tic, and when it was not repeated, decided that they had imagined the first outbreak.

When you have learned the mechanics of autocue, and seen how the behind-the-scenes bit of it works, move to the front of the camera. There you will find words scrolling up on a screen. You immediately feel that the words own YOU, as opposed to you owning the words. You have to go at THEIR pace.

"I was three years a newsreader before I suddenly realised that if I glanced away from the autocue screen for a moment, the words wouldn't go away," a friend of mine commented recently. "I had always operated on the assumption that I had to keep my eyes absolutely GLUED to the screen. Then I realised that I could glance away. Not only that, but I also realised that glancing away was making my autocue reading much more satisfactory, because it looked natural. It looked as if I was thinking the next thing, rather than just reading it at people."

There is a largely unappreciated significance to the fact that the devices used for this purpose on either side of the Atlantic are branded, respectively, as *Autocue* and *Teleprompter*. In neither case is the word "read" employed, because the correct use of the technology is to cue or prompt the speaker.

Good autocue users are those who know the general outline of their script, so that when the words come up on screen, they serve to remind the speaker of what he already knows, and act as a trigger propelling him into the next bit of information he wishes to offer for the audience's attention. The reader's eyes see a full sentence and he is able to tell that chunk of information to the camera. He can also glance away and "refer" to his script. The person watching feels communicated with, not impaled by a rigid stare.

The bad autocue user does not know his script and therefore has to read every word, discovering the collective sense of those words as he goes. Instead of *telling* the audience things, he reads necklaces of words at them, his eyes going from side to side and his face armoured with determination not to make a mistake.

Television people are often surprisingly dismissive about autocue-reading as a specific learnable skill. They talk about people as "good on autocue" or "bad on autocue" as if either were a genetic trait, like red hair. There is no genetic endowment giving some people talent in handling prompting technology, just as there is no genetic endowment related to bicycle riding. Practice makes, if not perfect, then as near as dammit to perfect.

During your preparation or rehearsal time in front of autocue, concentrate on these essentials:

* Reading from the middle or upper quadrant of the screen. Reading lower than that will make you look as if you are addressing your viewers' chins or bra straps.

* Using what is onscreen as a trigger

   Glance up. Take in the sentence. Tell it to the viewer. Don't raise your head and start reading—there is a difference, subtle but important, between the two.

Owning The Pace

Remember my newsreader friend who took three years to believe that he was in charge of the pace and that if he glanced away for a moment, everything would not disappear? Play games. Read as quickly as you can. The operator will stay with you. Now, read as slowly s you can. Do a big chunk slowly and then lash through a little bit. Still with you, see? The operator will stay with you, no matter what your pace. So vary that pace as much as you need to in order to inject interest into each succeeding piece.

Discovering the Content

Putting a script onscreen in front of you doesn't mean you can just bore us more fluently. We don't want to be bored at all. The fact that you have prompter technology in front of you is your private business. What we want in front of us is not a reader but someone whose way of talking suggests that hey, he has just come up with something he knows we'll find useful. We want someone who discovers things on the air with us, not someone who trails his monotonous way through the regurgitated secondhand discoveries in front of him.

Talking to One Person

Talking, not reading. To one person, not a cross-section of the vast public. Mrs Jones, drinking her cup of tea and watching the box, is not likely to be warmed and made happy by a TV personality who seems to be reading aloud words mysteriously printed across Mrs Jones cheekbones, instead of telling nice Mrs Jones, valued customer, a little secret that only the presenter knows.

Finally, remember writing for the spoken word. An autocue script will be seen by many people in the studio, and so the presenter is tempted to "tidy it up" and make it look more presentable. Don't. The autocue script should be in English you can talk, and laid out in the way that most helps you to talk naturally.

In both TV appearances and church sermons, one of the things that fascinates me about many religious is how happy they are to talk about areas of which they have no direct experience of—seminary life or living in a community. Thomas Kenneally's lovely *Three Cheers for the Paraclete* gives more fascinating insights into presbytery life than you will ever hear in a God Slot talk-to-camera, although the pressures and challenges of such a life would be much more interesting to lay people than inaccurately reflected versions of their own boring lives.

Politicians

If you want to be good at something requiring skill, you practice. If you want to be good at something technical which happens in a public or competitive arena, you get a coach. You pay that coach to alert you to elements in your performance which are detracting from the overall result, to catch you doing something right so that you can continue to produce that positive without its arrival being dependent on serendipity, and to push you to stretch your mental and physical capacities so that in a major event, all of your powers are under your control and you can be good. It can be swimming. It can be golf. It can be a team sport. The linked contribution of practice and a good coach is internationally acknowledged as an imperative. You don't win an Olympic medal by getting to the Olympic village, putting your runners on and doing your best.

Take the analogy over into the political arena, though, and the level of acceptance drops. If it is known that a particular politician rehearses before major television appearances, or works with a consultant who serves as a coach, it gives rise to a curious nudge-nudge, wink-wink fascination among observers. People tune in to see if they can spot the tricks. The idea that coaches might be working not to help the politician project a phony image, but to get his (or her) real self out there in front of the cameras is boring. Besides, there are lovely obvious examples of politicians being taught tricks. Saatchi and Saatchi fixed Maggie Thatcher's teeth and dropped her voice an octave, didn't they? Well, no they didn't, although they contributed to a change in image. I hope Saatchi and Saatchi are not as pursued by Maggie Thatcher's voice change as are the rest of us who consult with politicians. Because the voice she ended up with, although markedly less strident than the one she started out with, is artificial in the extreme and imitable by anybody who is not tone deaf, it serves as a constant distraction. It also leads to a public belief that consultants tinker with the political peripherals, getting people's teeth capped, stopping them saying "em" and solving the public perception problems of men like President George Bush.

In fact, according to Lilyan Wilder, the communications consultant acknowledged by Bush as a "constructive critic and outstanding coach," the President, when he first came to seek her advice, did so reluctantly, and in a state of extreme resistance to the notion of being "made over." Wilder watched him in action and told him he was a good communicator, pointing out his intrinsic strengths to him. She added that her function was to help him use those assets to the full.

"As we went over the practice videotape I'd made, I pointed out that his ideas could have been structured to come through more clearly. Excess verbiage and abrupt, unnecessary gestures were getting in the way of his message," recalls Wilder.

The man who was to become President decided, as a result of that first session, to make a serious investment of time in improving his public appearance skills. Within months, he had honed his skills in a way that allowed him to become freer and more spontaneous. Or, as Wilder puts it, "George Bush, who had been so sceptical, turned into a committed, enthusiastic student of oral communication."

Media people, whether they be presenters or reporters, tend to get ratty with the very idea of political coaching.

"No need for any of it," they say. "All a politician has to do is be honest and relax and he's going to have no problems."

Oh, yeah?

This advice is usually given by a TV professional who has:

- spent years coming to terms with nerves;
- total knowledge of the technology and crewing in the studio;
- a script sitting up onscreen in front of him, courtesy of the autocue operator;
- complete control over introductions, exit lines, questions and programme direction.

It is dead easy, from that position, to advise others to be

honest and relax.

What presenters and reporters are usually worried about is that the rehearsal has taught the politician how to tell credible lies and the coach has given the politician devilish tricks. I have been accused of this times beyond number, having, in the last decade and a half, trained politicians from five different political parties. The last time it happened, the journalist was naming names.

"Anybody can see the tricks you gave Mr X," she told me.

Tricks like what? I asked. (There is a great market for tricks, and if I was flogging them unbeknownst I could probably make more money by doing it with malice aforethought, not to mention a bit of direct advertising.)

"Oh, come ON," she said. "You know as well as I do."

I shook my head.

"He's different to what he used to be."

"So am I when I lose weight, but that's not a trick, that's called a diet," I said.

"OH, he's not thinner," she said, with an air of making a great concession. "But he's fluent. he's well informed. He doesn't get nervy any more. He talks sense."

I pointed out, with some asperity, that none of these accurate observations amounted to learned tricks. She conceded that with a grimace, but indicated that coaching which had those results had to be a trick. Or had to rely on tricks. Or something.

Good political communication does not need trickery. Good political communication is giving people understandable and useful information in a form they can remember and from the mouth of someone worth listening to.

This is not to say that there isn't lily-gilding going on behind a lot of political scenes. Close reading of the management of public image during the Kennedy Camelot days indicates that relatively little of what was published or spoken by JFK was originated by him. More recently, the Reagan era underlined that form can win out over substance. Gail Sheehy, the psychologist whose book, *Passages*, a decade ago examined the phases of human life, has, more recently, examined the character (or lack of it) attributable to various Presidential candidates coming up to the election which put Bush in the White House. Looking at the communications record of Reagan, Sheehy summed it up thus:

"Reagan's greatest gift is not verbal, it is the instinct for knowing how to make other people comfortable."

Whether at a dinner party, a public event or on TV, Reagan gave those present the impression that their company was brightening his day and that seeing them again would be even better—this despite the fact that he was known to have very few close friends and to spend most of his private time alone with his wife and dog. Reagan's lightness of touch, his desire to tell amusing stories and his deftness with a funny line, was cleverly built upon by his advisors in 1984, when, running against Walter Mondale, he fumbled a number of times and gave grounds for a rumour that he was ageing fast and less than competent for one of the world's most demanding posts.

The senility rumour threatened to get out of hand, and the President, as always, shrugged, smiled and waited for his advisors to suggest a line of response for the next public questioning. One was posited and rehearsed. In Kansas City, a brave journalist asked a question which took in the senility issue and Reagan duly "ad-libbed."

"I will not make age an issue in this campaign," he said softly. "I'm not going to exploit for political purposes my opponent's youth and inexperience."

Laughter in court. Nice filmed "bite" for that evening's news and other programmes for many other evenings. Senility ghost laid. Next question?

That is good preparation. That is building on a man's known capacities. That is answering a question in the only way it should be answered; a straight defence on the senility issue would not, could not work.

The media-management done for American presidents, and the realities of day-to-day political programming on this side of the Atlantic are widely different. In Britain and Ireland, political broadcasting, fortunately, has not followed the American model with the single exception, in Ireland, of the borrowing of the Big Debate format between the Taoiseach and the Leader of the Opposition. That single exception, with its clapometer trivialisation of what governing a country should be about, and its follow up in the following day's newspapers in graphs and minute by minute critiques which imply that good media performance equals good statesmanship, does no great service to democracy, although it may be good for ratings.

In general, politicians on this side of the Atlantic appear more frequently and in larger numbers for a greater length of time, interviewed by specialists who are well informed and more stringent than their transAtlantic counterparts. Although political broadcasting has improved in recent years (partly as the result of intervention by professional consultants and coaches, who have trimmed cliches, exposed lies and focused the thinking of speakers before the cameras roll), it is often bogged down because of politicians who play by dated rules.

An example is the advice "Don't let the other lot get away with anything" which seems to be graven on every politician's heart, and results only in a vicious circle of heckling which is disgusting to watch and unproductive to take part in.

Another is a blind unjustified fervour about that old chestnut "balance." Half the political world holds that balance in broadcasting is having one member of each party involved in every discussion, being introduced alphabetically, and given exactly the same time in which to speak. It sounds reasonable. Except that one politician who is good with words can unbalance an entire programme, even run on these rigid lines.

Politicians also tend to reach for infallibility as soon as they appear on television. They have never made a mistake. Their party has never made a mistake. Their mothers never made a mistake. Their grandmothers never... Consequently, viewers do not believe them, and tend to assume that valid claims of achievement are as false as the rest. The speaker who tries to seem infallible often leaves any chance of being engaging or forceful at the studio door.

On the other hand, it is important to be clear about what you want to say. Nobody in politics should be surprised into saying something they do not mean, or are likely to have to change their minds about, particularly since studies in America have shown that the public much prefers people who stick to the same belief throughout their career. It was said of Harold Wilson, for example, that he was never taken aback by what he was asked, and never tried to control it, as many politicians do, by demanding lists of questions in advance, or guarantees that they will not be asked particular questions. He knew roughly what areas were bound to turn up, listened for the key phrases, and said what he came to say. Edward Heath, on the other hand, regarded all interviews as war between himself and the interviewer, and it showed. The difference between the two men, as far as television was concerned, was that Wilson knew how to do it, and Heath was taking advice on how to do it. As commentator John Whale put it—

> From the moment Edward Heath became Conservative leader, he was beset with advice about how to behave on televisio, and, being a professional, he was disposed to take it. But there was so much of it that if he had taken it all he would never have been able to open his mouth; particularly since the common element was that he should start by effacing his own character.

There is a danger that with the involvement of public relations people, advertising consultants, and, God help us, communications consultants, politicians may become the creations instead of the creators. One Irish politician once asked me to identify for him what issues he should be seen to be identified with over the coming eight years. It is important to take good advice about radio and TV appearances. But it is also important a) to have a personal core and b) assimilate the advice so that it becomes your practice. Witness Whale's summation of Harold Wilson's TV persona—

> Like any good professional, he understood the given facts of the medium, technical and editorial, and was prepared to work within them. If a cameraman asked him to walk

down the garden steps from the cabinet room, cross the lawn and stop on a certain leaf facing in a certain direction, he did it without any sense of condescension, and got it right the first time. If it fell to him to begin some brief filming session by reading aloud the communique he was to answer questions about, he knew that he had to wait while the cameras were run up before he spoke. He knew it was an editorial requirement that his news broadcasts should be ostensibly addressed to a questioner and not to the world at large. He never tried, as some politicians did, to steal a look at the camera when he wanted to emphasise a point. He realised that the effect would be slightly disquieting, like an actor stepping outside his part in the theatre, and that it would probably be cut anyway.

True, many people did not like Wilson when he appeared, no matter how professionally he performed, either because they did not share his views or because they personally mistrusted him. That is another issue. What the politician in public wants to do is to be as effective as he/she can, based on whatever integrity he/she can muster.

It is obviously advisable, if you buy or borrow communications advice, that you get some which does not, like playing tennis with someone of a lower standard than yourself, leave you worse off than when you started. Ex-President Nixon's favourite media man was an "expert" named Murray Chotner, whose theory of political broadcasting went like this: Mobilise natural existing resentments by devising some organising principle for them; don't fight your actual opponent, create a straw man for that purpose; don't adopt any concrete position yourself, because it will merely afford openings to your opponent. People vote against, not for. (Quoted in *The Sunday Times*, August 11, 1974).

One area where experts can help enormously is the production of the party political broadcast. If they are allowed to; many politicians are rigidly convinced that the best party political broadcast is the one which has the politician face to camera, spouting his favourite speech. Talking heads are dull, and political talking heads are duller than most. In recent years, advertising agencies and independent film-makers have become increasingly sophisticated, technically and have much more variety of mood and style, ranging from the documentary to the animated fact-sheet. They still tend to rely too much on statistics, which neither prove nor disprove anything to the man or woman in the street, but they are getting better.

If you are involved in a "party political" then some points to watch for are these.

The background
Preliminary research by Dr David Canter at the University of Surrey in Guildford indicated that the background against which a party political programme is filmed is of great importance. Dr Cater filmed the same man making the same speech in front of three different backdrops. One was the exterior of a factory, one was a modern office, the third was the interior of a library. The library setting set off the best vibrations in people, the office the worst. People tended to feel that the man in the library was more pleasant, more active and more powerful than (the same) man in the office. He was also seen as more pleasant than the man outside the factory, but not necessarily as more powerful. The research is still at a preliminary stage, but the indications are that background is as important as, say clothes and hairdo.

The badges
It is not a good idea to have a lapel full of little symbols indicating that you are a member of Junior Chamber, Rotary, Women Against Violence Against Women, the Pioneer Total Abstinence Association, the blood donors or the nonswearer's league. The assumption that people will like you better because you are seen to belong to these is unjustifiable. Those who are not inclined to vote for you in the first place will be given more food for their fury. "Look," they'll yell, "the bastard's one of

those as well." The floating voters will spend more time trying to find out what the badges stand for than they will be listening to what you are saying. Unless you are talking about the organisation represented by the badge, do not wear the badge.

The way others see you/your party

By all means, be sensitive to the realities of your public image as a group. But do not go raking up accusations against yourself made by the other lot, unless they are major, current and immovably on everybody's mind. You are only reminding people of something they may otherwise forget.

On the other hand, if in the run-up to the election, the air around you has been thick with intrigue, double dealing and political assassination, do not appear with bags under your eyes down to your chest, blithely asking "Crisis? What crisis?

The committee instinct

Your party cannot broadcast. Only you can. That means that you must maintain a personal style and contact with the people you are talking to, instead of adopting a committee-like approach. Also, if your party wants lies told, get someone else to do it. Truth works better on television than lies. This is not an infallible rule—after all, the great American public was totally misled during the 'fifties by competitors in quiz games who agonised convincingly about knowing, or not knowing, the answers to questions which had seen secretly fed to them weeks beforehand. If you are cold, cynical and polished, then lies may be within your competence. If you are young, new to the game and reasonably idealistic, then do not be forced into being something you are not competent to be—a good stylish liar.

The political clichés

Just as the clergyman has ritual phrases which creep into the conversation unheeded, so have politicians. "The people of this great country," "Every right thinking person must agree," "A fair and frank exchange of views," are all such ritual noises. Buy a dictionary of clichés and add to it your own list of phrases you resolve to avoid henceforward. Because we are standing at a crossroads in our history, and if we do not pull up our socks, we may slide rapidly downhill.

Business People

Speakers from the world of business need to prepare for public speaking rather oftener than the rest of us, if only because they have so many publics. There is a general public, the business community, the shareholders, the consumers of their particular product, and a host of internal publics who appear at staff meetings and at presentations made within the company or to other companies.

In addition, there is a more widespread media interest in business than there was ten years ago. Now, there are weekly television programmes about management of money and about marketing. There are daily financial reports which include interviews, many of them live and conducted with someone on the end of a telephone. There are documentaries covering the latest buzzword area of management, whether it's MBWA or Corporate Culture.

A variation of the values system apparent in our view of politicians ("See how good he is as a TV debater, he would make a great President") obtains where business people are concerned. The woman who talks well at the annual management conference must be a great manager. The man who successfully mounts a TV defence of his company's survival plan, with its employment cutbacks, is seen as very much in charge. The man who sweats a bit and fumbles now and again as he is queried about a failed takeover is spoken of as an unlikely prospect for further career growth.

There is a new generation of Business Communicators. These are professional managers who rate communication as a crucial skill and as a personal priority. Lee Iaccocca's name is on two of the bestselling books which embrace this view, and the man who turned Chrysler around has made no secret of the fact that the corporate money he never minds spending is the finance required to train young executives to communicate well. The high profile success stories of Iaccocca and others have led many managers on both sides of the Atlantic to the conclusion that if you cannot communicate, you are unlikely to be a good manager.

Unfortunately, too many managers confine their idea of communication to the public arena. Every now and again, I will come across a man who has decided to devote a good deal of his costly time to learning how to make great speeches and surviving difficult interviews on television. He will rehearse endlessly, with and without autocue. He will answer all of the difficult questions put to him in a high-paced hostile manner. He will practice telephone-interviews until his handset shows signs of erosion. He may end up as publicly competent, or better, while never learning the basic skills of listening, of talking to staff so they understand the direction in which a company is driven, of participating in meetings—or chairing them so that business gets done, decisions are taken and individuals are not gratuitously crushed in the process.

One such business man is known within his company as Mr. Ed. Mr Ed, you may or may not recall, was a horse which gave the appearance of talking on television. This businessman was dubbed Mr. Ed because his staff saw him more often on TV than in reality, and because it was wondrous to them that he could appear to talk at all, since he did it so rarely and so badly within the company.

The direct opposite of the Mr Ed syndrome is exemplified by a chief executive who came to my company wanting a complete communications skills course.

"I want to know that I am competent to appear on TV," he said, in an oddly guarded way.

"That sounds as if you're not hungry to appear on The Box?"

"I hope I will never have to go on television," he said crisply. "But I want to have all the skills at my disposal, so that if I refuse or get someone else to do it, it isn't because of my inadequacy. My business will do nicely, thank you, without coverage, and I have no need for personal fame. Rather the reverse."

This man figured that while he learned about making presentations and appearing on television, he would also learn about himself and his patterns of communication within his company. He did. Before his training sessions, he had never seen himself on videotape. At his very first playback, he was startled to note how grimly threatening and contemptuous he looked when listening to a question.

"I often notice that people working for me get nervous when they have to talk to me," he said. "I've always thought they were just highly strung types and made judgements about their competence. Now I know why."

Not only did he learn how he looked and behaved, as that appearance and behaviour was viewed by someone else, he also learned how his company policy sounded to an external person. He developed radically different ways of articulating that policy, but he also in some instances changed it, on the basis that if he could not explain it to his own satisfaction in a controlled environment where there were no possibilities of negative leaks to media people, then there must be something wrong with it.

If this man is unlikely to go on television or radio, and unwilling to promote the possibility of an appearance on either medium, he is unusual within the business community.

Most business people quite like the idea of mediating their operations to the public on the small screen or through radio news programmes. Their PR advisers often explain that editorial coverage—that part of programming or print media which is not bought-and-paid-for advertising, is believed to a much greater extent than is even the best commercial. After some interesting media drubbings, Mobil decided that even the best-handled briefing tended, once a blue pencil or a video-editor's hands got to it, to be extremely believable to the viewers or readers, but to be carrying a skewed message from Mobil's standpoint. Mobil accordingly flew in the face of all of the usual advice favouring unpurchased "editorial" coverage, and ran a series of large advertisements on editorial pages of the classier newspapers, those advertisements frequently addressing issues, rather than selling petrol. In fact, as the series progressed, it emerged that selling product was NEVER a function of these ads. The function of the two-column ads was to give Mobil's corporate viewpoint on issues directly and indirectly related to energy supplies. The venture has been regarded as a pioneering breakthrough by business people who are less than trusting of media people, and as a profoundly nasty softening of the boundary line between objective editorial material written by an unbiased journalist on the one side, and subjective selling copy overtly tagged as such.

In Ireland and Britain, few PR consultants are so fearful of media that they advise against making an appearance which cannot be controlled by the businessman involved. There are some industries which are at best touchy when it comes to media because they believe that the media have been unfair in their treatment of their hiring practices, quality standards or the threats to the environment offered by their products.

"Why don't they treat us like the treat the electronic industry?" business people from one of the less "sexy" industries ask. "They treat them like *heroes*."

Public relations advisors, whether from within a company or from a retained consultancy, always try to explain the fashions in story-selection and why it comes about that one industry is semi-permanently topped with a white hat while another not only has a black hat, but horns and a tail to match. They regularly meet with the response "get out a statement." If a company makes an electric razor which is given to self-destruction when switched on, taking its owner, his designer stubble, his bathroom and a good portion of the neighbourhood into the wide blue yonder, that company is quite likely to hand the problem over to its public relations people with the request that they get out a statement.

These days, a statement is unlikely to fly on its own. Radio and TV will want a real warm body from the company, bringing the statement to life and answering questions about the problem. They will not accept a PR flak-catcher; they want a decision-maker. A decision maker who can handle media interviews can serve himself and his company very well during difficult times.

At a time of positive developments, when a company is launching a new product or bidding to take over some other corporate entity, PR consultants know from years of experience that placing a chief executive on a prime time television programme (assuming he handles the appearance with lucidity, if not panache or pizazz) creates clouds of kudos for the PR consultancy.

Very few businesses today can ignore the potential of good publicity. Very few. But there are some businesses which do not directly relate to the public, and which therefore have no need to put their chief executive on "talking head" television. If you are the chief executive in question and you want to go on television, you should be aware that your motivation is personal, rather than corporate, and that this very fact reduces your appeal to programme. In short, if your company is low profile and likely to remain so—why should you be high profile? The answer may be "because I'm a marvellous talker, because I have views on the wider business picture, and because I like public appearances." Fair enough. If you are NOT a marvellous talker, if you have no problems keeping your other views to yourself and if you hate the very idea of media interviews, then, like Brer Rabbit, you should lie low and say nuthin'. Do not buy the myth that media appearances are the ultimate justification for your existence.

If media appearances can do your business or your career some good, then they should not come about by accident. If they come about by accident, the accident will usually have negative connotations for you. In other words, you will be asked to appear on television because your balance sheet has hairy bits in it, because of industrial unrest or because of a product recall. Your role will be to explain things, and there is a certain truth to the old saw that "If you're explaining, you're losing." With the help of a good PR agency, on the other hand, you can plan a year's events which will give you good positive reasons for appearing on radio and television. If you want to do that, the key consideration is the need of the programmers. What do they need? What stories do they like? When is their best time? Meet the needs of the programmers, solve their problems, and you are likely to find yourself consistently welcome in radio and TV studios.

Business people should always be aware of jargon, which should be sliced away, and of cliches. One businessman never goes on TV without saying that his people are his greatest asset. If we believed it the first time around, and neither his workforce nor I did, we certainly don't believe it the tenth time around. Another comes from a company where if you don't talk about "synergy" every thirty seconds, you are looked upon as a heretic just waiting for an opportunity to renege.

Women

It may seen odd to give women a special segment to themselves, but in fact women have some specific problems to overcome in public appearances.

For generations, men have done women's speaking for them with notable exceptions like Nancy Astor, Countess Markievicz, La Pasionaria. Now that they are moving outside of their homes, becoming more politicised, joining organisations and often having to speak on their own behalf, they are finding that these decisions are not sufficient on their own to make them competent as public speakers. Many of them experience enormous fear—fear at a level many men would find difficult to credit. I have been involved in hundreds of communications courses over the past fifteen years, and organised roughly twenty five exclusively for women, and the single most obvious difference between the men (in general) and the women (in general) on the courses as been the fear factor. You say to a group of men that you are going to film them giving a five minute talk and they say "What do you want us to talk about?" the question carrying a happy assumption that even if you pick the topic for them, they will survive. Women, on the other hand, go silent, or say "Five minutes? I couldn't talk for five minutes. I couldn't talk for five seconds on a television."

Women's fears are also more likely to show up when the reality of a public appearance comes along. I have interviewed women whose hands shook so badly that they had to jam them between their knees to avoid being distracted by them, and the two people who fainted on me in radio studios were both women. This, despite the fact that both men and women instinctively prefer to watch a woman on television.

Women's fears about television are often justified. One of the reasons they are fearful is because they are so used to interruption.

Sociologists Candace West and Donald Zimmerman at the University of California, Santa Barbara, have done intensive study, using tape recordings of the pattern of conversation between men and women, and found that women are much more ready to be interrupted than men, and consequently are interrupted more frequently than they interrupt. One conversation taped by the sociologists went as follows:

Woman: How's your paper coming?

Man: All right, I guess. I haven't done much in the past two weeks.

Woman: Yeah, I know how that can—

Man: Hey, you got an extra cigarette?

Woman: Oh, sure. Like my pa—

Man: How 'bout a match?

Woman: Here you go, Uh, like my pa—

Man: Thanks

Woman: Sure I was going to tell you about my—

Man: Hey, I'd really like to talk but I've got to run. See you.

Woman: Yeah.

The sociologists who taped these conversations regard interruptions as part of a conversational politics women are not yet good at. Children are more interrupted by adults than interrupting (contrary to parental myth), and women are more interrupted because they feel more interruptible. Another American, looking at this type of finding, says that not only is the pattern of conversation capable of being modified, but that the very modification may change other aspects of women's lives. She is Dr Diane Horgan, assistant professor of psychology at Illinois State University—

"When women change the way they talk, they become more assertive around men. There's been a tendency for women to use words that connote an uncertainty, some doubt about their own statements, or words that don't convey any information."

Women going on radio or television should prepare carefully, as indicated elsewhere in this book. They should concentrate on content, not on nerves, on meeting the need of the audience and making the listeners feel informed and comfortable, rather than on removing the tremors from the backs of their own knees. And in preparing their material, they should think about some simple Don'ts and Dos:

Don't use expressions that imply uncertainty. "I'm not sure, and this is only my opinion, but it seems to m…"

Don't seek action weighing your argument with personal and emotional phrases.

"All of the indications are that this market has very little growth left in it, so the safe option is to wind down that operation," is a much more objective, less emotional way of stating a case than "I feel myself that we should wind down that operation because I don't think we'll get anywhere with it."

Don't seek permission to talk with questions like "D'you know what?" or "Could I put in a word here?" Just talk.

Don't make a statement and then tag a question after it. My husband says he will one day leave me for "statements" like "We'll have boiled eggs for tea. What do you think yourself?"

Don't assume that others have some divine right to speak, and therefore send out "please interrupt me" signals.

Do disagree if you feel like it. Some women will not do this in public because they feel it is not quite nice. Attack the argument, not the arguer and what you have is lively discussion, not a dogfight.

Do shave off the irrelevancies, like what year it was and where you were when someone said whatever it was to you.

Do prepare, so that when/if the presenter in a panel programme comes to you, you have something to say.

Emerging Specialities

As we go to press, there is a growing number of opportunities for experts in specialist areas to appear regularly and productively on radio and television. In many countries of the world, there are now consumer experts or car maintenance experts or gardening experts who have become household names because of their appearances on radio and television. On American radio at weekends, one of the most popular programmes, syndicated to stations across the nation, is one on car mechanics. For more than three hours, a car expert takes one phone call after another from people seeking advice on governors, valves and gears. He asks questions about cars which are sometimes two decades old, explores what remedial actions, if any, have already been undertaken and then comes up with recommendations on the air. He also introduces facts and news about cars and safe driving painlessly throughout the programme. Even if you take your car for granted and regard what's under the bonnet as a nasty possibility best confined to consenting adults like your local mechanic, you are likely to find this breezy unselfconscious expert a delight.

Local radio stations, particularly those in countries where the regulatory authorities insist on a public service component in the programming, have an increasing need for this kind of expert, in areas like health, industrial and domestic safety, child-care, DIY, gardening, Social Welfare entitlements, emotional problems, farming and a myriad of others. Television is likely to follow the same pattern, since the minicam and video technology have made on-location shooting so much cheaper than in the past. An expert can be brought to meet a group of questioners in a garden or a nursery school and 28 minutes of broadcastable television can emerge at relatively little cost.

All it needs is an expert who has a programme idea or an idea for an insert into a programme, a comfortable enthusiasm for sharing their information with others, and the willingness to prepare. Oh, and one other factor. If you are that expert, consider your light hidden under a bushel until you personally doff that bushel. Nobody in the TV or radio station knows that you are the talkative charmer you think you are until you tell them. And when you tell them, have the supporting evidence within easy reach.

Recommended Reading

1. Dr Robert Anthony, *How to Make a Fortune from Public Speaking* (New York 1983)

2. J A C Browne, *Techniques of Persuasion* (London 1967)

3. Patrick Campbell, *My Life and Easy Times* (London 1967)

4. Brian Cleeve, *Cry of Morning* (London 1971)

5. David Peoples, *Presentation Plus* (New York 1988)

6. Irving Stone, *Clarence Darrow for the Defence* (London 1969)

7. Robert Thouless, *Straight and Crooked Thinking* (London 1974)

8. Lilyan Wilder, *Professionally Speaking* (New York 1986)